I love this book for more reasons than I can list here. But all of them are related to Christy Berghoef's grounded humanity, her absolute integrity, her way of hallowing life's most ordinary experiences, and her capacity to look at life with both a critical eye and a compassionate heart—as when she writes about the mixed blessing called "community." To say nothing of her lucid and lovely prose. Early on in this book you'll benefit, as I have, from listening to a writer whose life and work are deeply rooted in the earth. "When the wisdom of the world is foolishness," she says, "the earth centers me on what is good and right and holy and wise." If you need that reminder as much as I do in these uprooted times, this is the book for you.

Parker J. Palmer, author of *Let Your Life Speak, A Hidden Wholeness,* **and** *Healing the Heart of Democracy*

Rooted is a love song for place and for renewed connection with land, creatures, family, and community—even when rebuilding those connections feels emotionally fraught. Christy Berghoef's gracious storytelling illustrates that sweat, love, and patience, when lavished on a beloved place, brings healing to heart and soul. This is a healing we need.

Debra Rienstra, author of *Refugia Faith*

Scientists can discern where a person grew up by the elements present in their bones. We carry our landscapes with us metaphorically but also quite literally. *In Rooted: A Spiritual Memoir of Homecoming,* Christy Berghoef beautifully describes what it means to have a deep and abiding sense of place and how the experience of home and homecoming can go bone deep. She invites us to walk with her along the muddy creeks and hardwood stands of West Michigan, catch glimpses of the holy while washing dishes, to kneel and lay our hands on the good earth and feel the power of its healing presence. Berghoef's memoir recounts her own spiritual journey as one of leaving an exclusive religiosity, and finding another kind of homecoming in a more expanded, living, breathing faith experience of love made visible in every daily action. *Rooted* is a testament to the holy and hard, a keenly perceptive woman's embodied experience with love, loss, and the everlasting, and an invitation to walk through our own histories and homecomings with a sense of wonder, gratitude and grace. *Rooted* is a gift in a weary world that so needs the spirit this book offers and the wisdom it contains.

Carrie Newcomer, musician, poet, and author of *The Beautiful Not Yet* and *A Great Wild Mercy*

Those of us lucky enough to have known a place and a community well and deeply will recognize all the joys and complications in this book; for others, it will be an eye-opening and heart-opening account of what's still possible in this country.

Bill McKibben, environmentalist and author of *Wandering Home*

We learn how to love from people who love well. At a time when disregard for the earth and its web of life has been normalized, *Rooted* tells a compelling, informed, deeply personal love story. Without a shred of sentimentality, it traces one woman's return to the forty acres generations have cared for and her moments of reawakening to the vibrant life on it, its resilience and variety, and what she learns about how to love it well with a fierce love that grows the spirit, sustains resolve to care for fellow creatures, and teaches her how to protect and preserve what has been given. Some books bless us as we read them. This is one of those.

Marilyn McEntyre, author of *Caring for Words in a Culture of Lies*

I've always liked how the Bible says we are "working out our salvation with fear and trembling." It reminds me that true salvation, coming from the root meaning "salve," is about healing, and it's not just a moment but a process. This is a beautiful, salvific book by a wonderful child of God on a journey of healing and homecoming. May it encourage you on your own salvation journey, as we work to heal all that is broken in our hearts, in our streets, and in our world.

Shane Claiborne, author, activist, and co-founder of Red Letter Christians

Maya Angelou says the ache for home lives in all of us. This is true even when home gets complicated, even when we must grapple with who we've been and who we're becoming. Amid Christy's lyrical, gritty prose, my ache grows stronger. And my hope for all of us to find our deep home rekindles.

Winn Collier, Director of the Eugene Peterson Center for Christian Imagination and author of *Love Big, Be Well* and *A Burning in My Bones: The Biography of Eugene H. Peterson*

Honest, funny, touching, insightful, and richly descriptive. This memoir by Christy Berghoef is a must-read for anyone who realizes we need to take better care of our home planet.

That should include everyone. Through engaging personal stories in wonderful prose, this book is a beacon of profound hope. Take up and read.

Steve Bouma-Prediger, Professor of Religion at Hope College and author of *For the Beauty of the Earth: A Christian Vision of Creation Care* **and** *Creation Care Discipleship: Why Earthkeeping Is An Essential Christian Practice*

In this frenzied, threatening time, many talk about the need to be grounded. And as climate catastrophes impinge on our daily lives, afflicting the poor most severely, many talk about recovering a sacred connection to the earth. When Christy Berghoef returned home to West Michigan years ago, she began living a grounded life rooted to the earth. This book shares the power of her lived experience. It demonstrates Christian faith rooted, not in the head, but in the heart, and with the earth. And she writes with lyrical beauty. What a joy to read.

Wesley Granberg-Michaelson, General Secretary emeritus of the Reformed Church in America and author of *The Soulwork of Justice*

Rooted

A Spiritual Memoir of Homecoming

Christy Berghoef

For more information and a free downloadable discussion guide, visit:

ReformedJournal.com/all-books

Cover photo by Christy Berghoef
Cover design by Rick Nease
RickNeaseArt.com

Published by Reformed Journal Books
Publishing services provided by Front Edge Publishing
42807 Ford Road, No. 234
Canton, MI, 48187

Front Edge Publishing books are available for discount bulk purchases for events, corporate use, and small groups. Special editions, including books with corporate logos, personalized covers, and customized interiors are available for purchase. For more information, contact Front Edge Publishing at info@FrontEdgePublishing.com.

Contents

For Dad—

Bent low to the earth,
your hands touched the soil
not to command,
but to commune.

You showed me that every furrow is a prayer,
every seed a quiet promise—
that the earth holds more than roots:
it holds remembrance, hope, and grace.

You taught that true strength
is found on its knees,
in the humility of care,
in the patience of tending.

This is for your sacred labor,
your open hands,
and the future you nurtured
with steadfast love and quiet faith.

About the Cover

The cover image was taken on a foggy morning at the farm where I grew up—a place rooted in love, hospitality, and quiet generosity. At the center of the scene is a small hill rising behind a still pond. Decades ago, my father planted three trees there, drawn by the spiritual resonance of "three trees on a hill." On this morning, veiled in fog, the hill and its trees appear both softened and luminous, their reflection mirrored perfectly in the pond below—real and yet ethereal.

This image captures the essence of the story told within these pages: a spiritual memoir about returning home, both literally and inwardly. After years spent in a wider world that reshaped my beliefs and worldview, I moved back to the land of my childhood. In addition to a U-Haul packed with my belongings, I carried the weight of fear—fear of being judged or rejected for who I had become. But the forty acres of the farm embraced me without hesitation. Though the broader community often held me at arm's length, the land welcomed me with a familiar grace. The fog in the photograph speaks to the uncertainty of that return; the trees, to enduring love, and the reflection, to the way the past and present can finally see each other clearly.

This cover is more than an image. It is a homecoming.

Christy Berghoef, summer 2025, **christyberghoef.com**

Foreword

Like Christy Berghoef, I spent my earliest years "in the country," as opposed to the city or the suburbs (which were a new thing back then). When she tells stories of chasing elusive butterflies among the flowers, finding crayfish under rocks—waving their pincers in warning—or picking up wriggling snakes and slippery frogs in the meadow, I can feel those memories awaken in my body.

When I was about to start school, we moved to a town where streets were straight, blocks were rectangular, and sidewalks lost their battle with the underlying roots of elm and maple trees. My great compensation was that about four doors down the street stood the public library. That's where I gained my love of books. Every week (in my memory, at least), my mom took my brother and me to trade in the books we had read and re-read the previous week for new ones, and all for free!

I have been a reader ever since. I love all kinds of books: geeky books by specialists who stretch my ability to understand, funny books that give me permission to laugh at the pretentious folly of the powerful, books that nourish my spirit and remind me of the depths that underlie the daily barrage of distraction, books that help me cope with whatever is overwhelming me.

Near the top of my list of "love to read" books are those that simply help me feel more fully alive.

That's what drew me to Christy Boerghoef's beautiful new memoir, *Rooted*.

There's a lot of madness overheating the world at this moment. There's a lot that makes us feel afraid, terrified even … a lot that makes us feel angry, outraged even. When you find a writer who helps you descend beneath the turbulence and find some stillness, what Howard Thurman called "the sound of the genuine," you know that you have found a treasure.

There's a lot to be said for writing that is both sane and savory, that will help you survive and catch your breath. *Rooted* is that and does that, and it does so by taking you back home—to childhood, adolescence, your first job, your first child, your most awkward transitions, your moments of transcendence and triumph.

You may have grown up in a suburb full of cul de sacs or a city laid out on a grid. You may have grown up on the twentieth floor of a high-rise apartment building rather than a West Michigan flower farm. But wherever you grew up, you faced the challenges along with the blessings of having a family. You faced the perplexities of learning to navigate a great big world and of learning to inhabit a changing body.

You survived the bafflements of religion and other institutions that sometimes helped you and sometimes boxed you in.

Christy tells her story in a way that will help you get in touch with your own, and it will help you understand *home* as never before. Homespun yet beautifully crafted, *Rooted* will bring healing and a smile to the deepest parts of you.

I've had the privilege of knowing Christy and her family for a couple of decades now, and I've grown to respect her as a genuine writer, a skilled photographer, and a wise human being. I'm so glad you'll get to know her when you turn this page.

Brian D. McLaren
May 2025

Introduction

I had two celebrity crushes in high school: the novelist-essayist-poet-farmer Wendell Berry and the travel writer and TV host Rick Steves.

Wendell Berry's work pointed to the sacredness of the ground beneath me. According to Berry, I had everything I needed where I already was—I didn't need to go someplace else to discover myself, I needed to bloom where I had been planted. I loved Wendell Berry. But I also loved Rick Steves, whose Saturday afternoon *PBS* travel show opened an untapped vein of curiosity about a world wider and more wondrous than our small family farm.

Stay or go?

I wanted both.

I never wanted to leave home and never wanted anything to change. I loved the land where I lived and, in the spirit of Wendell Berry, wanted to bloom where I had been planted. Yet I also couldn't wait to get away. I wanted to explore new places with different people, different cultures, different foods, different geography, different languages, different architecture, different theologies, different politics, different religions. I wanted to know more of all our planet held.

After attending a Christian high school and Christian college close to home, I branched out into the world and moved from West Michigan to Washington, D.C. I was committed to making a difference in the world working for a Republican congressman. While living and working in Washington, things happened that changed the trajectory of my life.

As a result of a study trip to Israel/Palestine with one of my former high school teachers, my faith started to move from being a set of static theological points to something living and breathing, something alive in the world. I'd been raised in a religious tradition where the head ruled the heart and had more or less thought that if I believed the right things, I would spend eternity in a mansion on a street paved with gold, with a zero-maintenance perfectly landscaped yard and lake frontage. Once there, I would be surrounded by PLMs, People Like Me, people who shared my theology, people who shared my politics, people who shared my views on social issues. Up there on the lakefront, we'd be spared everlasting eternal conscious torment in a different kind of body of water—a sea of flames that perpetually burned but never killed. All those trapped in the sea of flames had made a grave error: they believed the wrong things. As a result they were damned to eternal punishment by our loving but just God whose fury was reserved for unfortunate souls who got their theology wrong.

As my world and worldview expanded, I began to focus my religious understanding on the present world. Jesus, I came to see, was calling me to a life that recognized the hells of the world right here and right now and his life and teaching was compelling me to be part of bringing justice, peace, and wholeness to such hellish places. I began to realize I had spent my life judging others from a place of both privilege and ignorance. I was no longer finding purpose working on Capitol Hill—I wanted to serve in some capacity beyond politics. After a year in D.C., I moved back to Michigan and enrolled in my denomination's seminary.

I met my husband, Bryan, at Calvin Theological Seminary. After graduation and marriage, we began a life of church planting. Our first church plant was in Traverse City, Michigan. It was a time of immense spiritual growth and development, which at times was painful. (Those years were the subject of my previous book, *Cracking the Pot*.) These days, we call what I went through "deconstruction," which sounds like a negative way of saying I was growing. I was moving away from childhood certainty to a more complex faith. Outside the bubble where I'd been raised, there was no denying that the religious rules I had championed simply didn't work for many people. In fact, many of the rules that benefitted me often led to worsening circumstances for others.

More change happened as we had four children during those years. The church began to really take off and this created a crossroads moment for Bryan and me. Our calling was to plant churches, not maintain them. We began looking for a new ministry challenge.

With the blessing of our denomination, we left Traverse City to plant a church in Washington, D.C. I was excited to head back east, this time with Bryan and our children. Once there, my experience was much different than it had been during my days on Capitol Hill. I saw life through the eyes of our children, who were enrolled in public schools alongside kids with heartbreaking stories. Once again, the assumptions I'd grown up with were challenged. For example, I had naïvely assumed people got what they deserved in life. I grew up believing you reaped what you sowed. If someone was poor, it was likely their own fault. But in Washington, I saw firsthand that the hardest working people often lived in the most dire circumstances. They planted and planted and planted but rarely enjoyed a harvest. I began to appreciate that people were often powerless in the face of larger systems.

Our neighborhood was diverse in every way imaginable. Across the street from our house were homes with cracked windows and bed sheets for curtains. Just down the street were small family restaurants and low-income housing complexes. A block behind us were embassies and large estates. We were in the middle of it all. Fabulous backyard parties brought our neighbors and us together across differences.

Rather than work on Capitol Hill, I worked a couple part-time jobs for faith-based organizations: one, a nonprofit working on issues of mass incarceration and the inherent racism embedded in our criminal justice system, the other working with members of Congress building bridges across the divide between Republicans and Democrats. That divide was expanding. The Tea Party was on the rise and congressional members were discouraged—even punished—for building relationships with those across the aisle. The expectation was that members would align themselves completely with their party leadership. Compromise—a hallmark of effective leadership in a democracy—was going out of style.

I had the opportunity to work with the late Congressman John Lewis, a giant figure in the American Civil Rights movement. In 2013, when the Supreme Court gutted the Voting Rights Act, which a young John Lewis had literally had his head cracked open working for, I saw a deep-seated callous racism within the Republican Party. The very next day many Republican-controlled state legislatures began implementing policies that would put up roadblocks between people of color and the voting booth. I grew disillusioned and deeply troubled. I was far from the idealistic young Republican I'd been when I originally came to Washington.

How much had I changed? In 2004, I'd been backstage with George W. Bush at a presidential debate. In 2013, our family joined the throngs who stood in the cold, lining Pennsylvania Avenue, cheering the second inauguration of President Barack Obama.

Yet as all this was happening, there were significant issues. It was hard to gain traction with our church plant in D.C. The people we attracted were young and transient and there weren't enough resources to pay us adequately, especially since the cost of living in D.C. was astronomical. To support ourselves, Bryan worked full time for a nonprofit and I worked two part-time jobs. We raised funds and did church things on evenings when we didn't have work events. Weekends were focused on church gatherings that took place in our living room. Exhaustion was creeping in fast and hard, but we didn't see it coming until it had us pinned to the ground almost unable to move. We were burnt out on the church, and decided to leave ministry.

The last straw came when one of our boys was diagnosed with severe dyslexia and his school lacked the resources to adequately help him. Our son's educational needs became our top priority.

We could work our jobs remotely (the other jobs we held, the ones which actually paid us), and so the whole country was open as we sought the best learning environment for our son. Where would we go next? The number one school option, an option that kept popping up as we researched, was a little school in Michigan with a remarkable teacher who had great success with kids with learning differences.

Of all the places in the large state of Michigan, the school was in my hometown.

We needed to go home.

Home.

I was terrified. It was nearly impossible to imagine dragging our exhausted bodies back to the most politically and theologically conservative pocket of the state of Michigan. I recalled the way my community had treated people who didn't see the world like they did. People like the person I had become. I almost couldn't breathe as I thought of the kind of cruelty our family could potentially be subjected to.

I'd spent my adult life getting out of that place. Now I was going back. It was time to embrace my inner Wendell Berry and see if I could bloom where I had originally been planted. Could I take root and grow there now that I was a different person? Thomas Wolfe famously said you can't go home again. I was about to find out if that was true.

In the 1940s, my grandparents left South Dakota and bought an old farmhouse on forty acres south of Holland, Michigan. As they grew older, they cut off a corner of the farm and built a small house to retire in. My parents moved into the big farmhouse. I was three when that move happened. My family didn't have much—I wore my brother's hand-me-downs, the house's plaster was cracked and crumbling, and the wallpaper peeled in the corners. But we had those beautiful forty acres. Eventually, my dad started a business raising flowers, and I grew to love and know the land. After my grandparents died, my parents bought the little house and rented it, hoping that one day one of their children would live in it. That day had come.

Our family of six moved into my grandparents' small house on the ground of my childhood. We put our roots down where I had grown up. Thank God we did. Over and over again, it was that ground that saved me, rescued me, and provided promise and comfort throughout the hardships that lay ahead. The earth saved me from the world.

In these pages, I make a distinction between the "earth" and the "world." Here's one way to think of that distinction: The earth is what God has made and the world is what humans have made. The earth has much to teach us about living in the world and I have found that I cannot endure the world without being close to the earth. When I sit too long with the harsh realities of the world and become distant from the earth, discouragement overwhelms me. I have to be rooted in the earth to live in the world.

What follows are a series of stories of what it was like to come home as I embraced the earth and made my way in the world. Before jumping in, it's important to name two additional things. First, the land I live on once was home to the Odawa and Potawatomi tribes. In 1849, sensing that their way of life was threatened by a growing immigrant population (my people) and the smallpox epidemic the immigrants brought with them, the tribes were forced to move to northern Michigan. The land I call mine was the sacred land of their community. They had an intimate relationship with it long before I did.

Second, I recognize the incredible privilege of having easy access to a truly stunning forty acres. The fact that I'm able to step out back for a stroll through the woods, across hills and fields, along trickling streams, and around the pond any time I'm feeling a little stressed is not something everyone can do. I feel this privilege profoundly. I have an intimate relationship with the same piece of land that my father knew well and his father before him. Now my children know it, too. This is a rare and precious gift that I will never take for granted.

My hope is that by sharing my story, you are inspired to a place of awe and wonder. I hope you'll attune yourself to the wisdom the earth whispers. And my prayer is this compels you to open your heart with greater compassion for the world.

Homecoming

My eyes blurred and cleared intermittently for the first several hours of the drive from Washington, D.C., to Holland, Michigan. They filled, then overflowed. Filled, then overflowed again. Bryan was driving the U-Haul crammed with beds, tables, outdoor furniture, and boxes of the things we deemed worth dragging across the country. I followed in the Odyssey toting all four kids and a few precious items that we didn't want bouncing around in the back of the truck. We white-knuckled our way out of the D.C. morning rush, a stressful route even on a normal day.

The community with whom I felt absolute belonging, despite all our differences and our variety of views, grew smaller and smaller in my rearview mirror until it vanished completely. That's the moment it began. My lungs sucked and expelled air in fits and starts while I wept as if someone had not only opened a hose, but walked away and forgotten about it, leaving an expanse of puddles and squishy pools across the lawn.

The kids were silent. Eerily silent. Quite possibly more silent than four kids aged five through ten confined to car seats have ever been in the history of road trips. *They are respecting my grief*, I told myself. More likely they were terrified and traumatized by the length and loudness of my wailing. They had never seen me broken down like this. *They are going to need therapy*, I told myself.

Somewhere just into Pennsylvania the well ran dry. I was empty, dried out like a Southern California reservoir after a ten-year drought. As if waiting for this moment, Winston, my nine-year-old, found the courage to lift his voice onto the stage of silence. "Um, Mom? I really have to pee. We have to stop."

I called Bryan in the U-Haul to let him know. We exited just before the Pennsylvania Turnpike to stretch our legs, empty our bladders, and fill our gas tanks and stomachs. My cheeks were like fat warm tomatoes fallen from the vine, not just absorbing the heat of mid-August on the top side but enduring the scourge of decay on the underside. Streaked with salt, the flesh around my eyes was tender and swollen. More than a few folks in the bustling gas station looked on with pity. I assumed they thought we were traveling for a funeral. Or is this just what a woman travelling across the country with four kids in a minivan looks like?

My stomach was too tight and sour and my mouth too dry to be able to eat anything. I opted for orange juice to go. The kids, still tiptoeing around me but clearly happy to be out of confinement, feasted on gas station cheeseburgers and chocolate milk. Before strapping back in for the next leg of the drive, I did some deep breathing and stretching in the parking lot while they ran up and down a small patch of green lodged between the parking lot and the gas station.

After another hour on the road, with me presenting a calmer and more normal version of myself, the kids began getting fidgety and cranky. "How long till we get there?" I was tempted to remind them that back when I was their age, our family of six had to cram into a little 1968 Honda N600 to get anywhere. My two older brothers jostled in a cramped tight backseat, and I sat on pillows on top of the parking brake lever between the front bucket seats while my one-year-old brother climbed around the car like a fat little caterpillar. He wriggled in and out amongst us as he pleased, jabbing with a wild foot or stray elbow from time to time. We were just grateful to be alive in the era of motorized vehicles. I was tempted to say it, but instead slid *The Lion, The Witch and the Wardrobe* audiobook into the CD player to settle them down for the duration of the trip. The kids had listened to this so often they had much of it memorized and frequently spoke the lines aloud in unison with the reader.

The next few hours on the road felt as if I was outside of my body and moving through a tunnel on autopilot. I was traveling through the wardrobe and I wondered if in time I would entirely forget the world I was leaving behind and all I had known and learned there. I wondered if the various ways I had grown would shrivel up and leave me shrinking back down into my old self.

The landscape outside the window became like one long ribbon caught in the breeze streaming in a blur alongside us, and the storybook began to dwindle down to a smudgy smear of sound. After the long slog through Ohio, we crossed under the big blue "Welcome to Pure Michigan!" sign, and I

was jolted to full wakefulness by the notoriously hardscrab-
ble Michigan highways, which tossed the van around as if
we were driving down a rough gravel road. My mind began
racing. *What are we doing here? Will they even want us back
home?* All my fears and questions were met with silence as I
dodged six-inch-deep potholes. *We should have moved somewhere else.* I wondered if this pocked warzone road was a
warning.

The kids began whooping it up in the back of the van.
They were eager to live two flower fields and one alfalfa field
away from Grandpa and Grandma and closer to their cousins. In D.C., we lived on a busy street: Sirens screamed day
and night and shouting voices swam from open windows
across the thick hot soup of summer night air. The ability to
roam the wild country would be a welcome contrast. In the
thrill of adventure, they seemed easily able to embrace what
was ahead and set aside the sadness of missing their friends
and neighbors.

I decided to make an effort to meet them in their enthusiasm. I began the work of burying my grief, fears, and
hesitation in order to dig out the little pockets of hope that
were hidden inside me. I joined them in pronouncing all
the great things that were waiting for us in Michigan. Open
fields. Fresh air. Small town. Minimal traffic. Great schools.
A yard. A garden. Lake Michigan. Grandpa and Grandma.
Sublime, sacred silence.

Maybe this would all be okay after all.

The more mile markers the minivan trundled past, the
more both my hopes and fears expanded inside me, while
my breath felt squeezed out of my conflicted lungs. The

confused state of my insides started spinning, bordering on nausea.

Would the place and people of my hometown ever allow me to really feel at *home?* I was no longer part of the tribe. I knew that. While my values hadn't changed, the political expression of those values had shifted. This would be enough to make for a thorny existence in a conservative community. I knew this because there was a time when I was part of the hometown crowd that demonized people who were exactly like the person I had become. Being politically liberal was a grave sin, and I was sure the wider community would tell me in a variety of ways that I was unwelcome, unwanted, and outside the grasp of God's grace.

The increasing joy and excitement on the four little faces bobbing around in my rear-view mirror offset my doubts and angst. Somewhere on Interstate 96 I resolved to endure anything as long as my kids were okay. Keeping them feeling safe, loved, valued, and nurtured would be my goal. I gripped the steering wheel and found myself praying that the challenges of coming home would not shatter their sweet enthusiastic spirits.

The landscape outside the window started to become familiar: like an old acquaintance at first, then like a long-time friend, and as we were pulling into a gravel driveway as familiar as family. We were home. The garage door was a mosaic of "Welcome Home" messages from my niece and nephews. An unexpected surprise for the kids. A wee little seed of hope pressed into the soil of my mind.

We climbed out of the van and stretched the crimps out of our muscles. Squealing, the kids skipped quickly inside like little grasshoppers. The screen door creaked open and slapped shut behind me. This was the house that would be our home. The home that my grandparents built and lived in during the latter half of their lives. The home that sat at the edge of the forty-acre farm my dad grew up on, that I grew up on, and where my parents still lived.

I was flooded with the warmth of nostalgia. It was unexpected. My dried-up eyes started to draw from a restocked reservoir. My memory called up the lingering scent of date-filled cookies, moth balls, Grandpa's Big Chief chewing tobacco, and Grandma's Avon skin cream. How were these scents so palpable, given that Gramps and Grams had been gone for years? Their smells must have saturated the carpet, soaked into the walls.

I swear I could see my grandfather's bony frame tucked into the corner of the room, sunk in his brown recliner, a stack of books beside him on the table, checkerboard—cracked at the seams and repaired with layers of brittle masking tape—lying open and ready on the leather footstool. He looked up and called out to me, "Christy Rae! I've been waiting for you. Let's go! The board is ready!" I could hear him as he always was. I could hear his voice coming from his corner of the room, through his nearly toothless grin, wet tobacco wad set on the coaster on the table beside him. I squeezed my eyes against the tears trying to escape, aching to turn back the years to simpler times when the world seemed a small and straightforward place, to sit at his feet and wait for him to slide the first worn wooden checker across the board.

Home.

Everything looked the same. Dark sienna living room carpet with smudges of rust color worked in. Dark walnut cabinets with brass handles straight out of the 1970s lining both sides of the tiny galley kitchen. I moved down the hall and peeked into the small bathroom. Mustard yellow tub and golden yellow floor tiles, just as it had always been. One bedroom with lime green shag carpet that was all the rage in 1978 and a second bedroom with a more updated cream-colored Berber carpet. The kids scrambled downstairs to run around the wide-open unfinished basement. Winston shouted from the bottom of the stairs, "We can ride our scooters and rollerblade down here!"

I smiled at the thought and moved through the kitchen and out the back door. Stopping just beyond the edge of the yard, I kicked my shoes off, stepped into the field, and sunk my cramped, caged feet into the warm, just-turned soil of the back forty. Robins and blue jays were chattering wildly in the black walnut trees. Song sparrows fluttered at the bird feeder. I gazed across the field where acres of gladiolus were cracking through the soil and my eyes lifted to the woods beyond. As I inhaled slowly and deeply, the sun-warmed soil wrapped itself around my feet and the breeze threw open its arms as if to say, "Welcome home." I let myself fall fully into this unconditional embrace.

The earth knew me. A voice from somewhere whispered to my heart that this patch of earth would love me, accept me, and understand me just exactly as I was, in all my circumstances, regardless of how I fared in the world. Fresh air moved over the alfalfa field, carrying a hint of the neighbor's milk cows with it before flowing easily and fully through my lungs. My clenched muscles relaxed and eased. All my twisted, anxious nerves unfurled.

This was the ground that had birthed me, nurtured me, and held me all those years. I knew for certain this ground would hold me still. As I was easing myself into place, a small cloud of dust rose in the distance. I squinted as Mom and Dad emerged, rumbling across the field on the Gator toward us. The kids ran from the house squealing as their grandma and grandpa approached the yard. A smother of lanky little arms and legs wrapped around my parents like kite string knotted around a willow branch, and they were buried in affection. As that tight knot of love began to dissipate, Mom and Dad looked beyond my children to me, their open arms ready to embrace. I made my way across the yard and fell into them.

I was home.

2

The Holy Gospel of Dust

I lay in bed on that first summery morning home as a deluge of early morning light poured through the window and floated across the bedroom. Here, away from screaming sirens and roaring traffic on the busy D.C. street where we had lived. Here, where mourning doves and song sparrows compete for attention in the black walnut trees and the air carries a pleasant nip and slight crispness.

Comfortable sleeping weather, we call this.

Bryan was still on his back, asleep. He exhaled slowly and steadily, sending waves of movement through the air as tiny dust particles illuminated by the early light swirled and surfed on the warm current of his breath.

In that moment of steady breathing and morning light, I slipped into a state of spiritual, emotional, and physical quietude. Everything around me and everything within me seemed aware and fully present to the moment. The universe inside me and the world around me were perfectly still and perfectly attuned.

Deep memory suddenly overwhelmed my body.

The old farmhouse was drafty. The windows, thin and full of rippled imperfections. Michigan winter was persistent in knocking on the doors and rattling the windows, always begging to get inside, and cleverly finding ways to penetrate the thick walls or slip through the small cracks that were apparently everywhere.

Dad kept the house warm by feeding chopped pine, ash, and maple into the stomach of the roaring woodburning stove. We all had to take turns swinging the axe, splitting logs Dad had sliced from felled trees, to be sure the covered red wagon stayed full of winter fuel. It served to keep the heart of our home toasty. But the chill of outside seemed to always find a way to seep through invisible pores of the creaky old house, dissipating the warmth in the far rooms and edges of our home. My bedroom was upstairs and well within that chill zone.

The coldest wintry nights had me buried under so many heavy layers of thick blankets that at times I could barely lift my chest high enough to squeeze the necessary oxygen into my lungs. I might as well have been strapped down, because it took effort even to roll over under the weight of so much cotton and wool. As long as I remained cocooned and didn't wriggle free, exposing myself to the cold, I usually managed a full eight hours of nightly hibernation.

The walls of my bedroom were covered with a popcorn-textured white paint. My bedspread had been stitched with care by my mom, along with matching curtains out of a pretty red and white gingham fabric. Mom had managed to salvage enough scraps to sew a matching sleeper for my doll, Sally, as well. In my short doll-loving phase, Sally was always tucked in beside me at night.

The speckled walls of my bedroom had cracks and holes and patched-up spots. As I lay waiting for sleep to take me, my mind would connect the tiny bumps on the walls like a limitless dot-to-dot in a coloring book or a night sky full of unnamed constellations. Entire creative worlds would unfold in my imagination around my island of red and white gingham. Sometimes I imagined my walls were stretches of sand laid out around me as far as I could see, and I was an adventurer caught in the middle of the Sahara Desert. I could only hunker down and let sleep take me until the wind died and the dust settled.

At the foot of my bed hung a picture my grandma had painted for me. Two little yellow-haired children in matching cornflower blue and spearmint green footie pajamas were down on their knees, each with their hands pressed together in perfect prayer poses. Words were inscribed in the space between them:

> Angel of God, my guardian dear,
>
> to whom God's love commits me here,
>
> ever this day be at my side,
>
> to light, to guard, to rule and to guide.

Words at the foot of your bed nearly always stay with you, especially if you're one who doesn't fall immediately asleep. This painting hung on my wall before I could read, and these words were some of the first words I learned to sound out. Angels, love, and God as my guardians were not a bad thing to have on my mind as I drifted off every night, particularly stuck in the middle of the desert as I sometimes was.

The icy winter mornings always came charging rudely into my dreams. First the alarm. Then wriggling my hand free from the layers to slam off the steady, snapping, whining beep. Next came the awareness that my nose was an ice cube, followed by the ritual of cupping my hands over my mouth and nose for a few moments, pushing out moist warm morning breath into the cavity of my hands to thaw the numbness. The heated carbon dioxide rolled from my lips like puffs of smoke as it folded into the chilly air of my room. In a minute or two, I would work up the bravery to hoist myself out from under the covers, dash across the icy floorboards, snatch my clothes for the day in a quick swipe, and make my way downstairs to the warm heart of our home.

The fire often went out at night, but Dad would already be there, scooping out the mound of cold ashes from the prior day, carefully preserving a few hot lumps and strategically piling up the kindling for fresh heat as I made my way down the creaky, steep, narrow stairwell. It would take some time for the heat to warm through the thick iron of the stove. As I waited, I would spread my clothes on the bricks surrounding the stove to warm them as the fire approached a nice roar.

On those occasional winter mornings when the sun decided to stretch itself out from beneath Michigan's often cloudy gray sky, the light of the sunbeams would throw itself across the living room floor through the tall leaded east-facing windows. There was warmth in the sunbeam. And a good measure of comfort. I would lie on my back in the light on the floor, wrapped in a blanket crocheted by my mom's mom—the grandma I never knew—and settle into a moment of what I came to think of as my "warm place of waiting."

Waiting for the house to warm.

Waiting for my clothes to warm.

Waiting for the start of whatever this new day held.

With my body curled up where the light hit the floor, I would quietly watch the dust in the air, ignited by the great aurora happening in our living room, as it floated, swirled, and drifted on the hot currents.

The dust shimmered with an aliveness as the small silvery specks curled, whirled, and rolled around like miniature ballerinas in whimsical unchoreographed movement, each one moving independently, yet somehow embodying the ineffable in the mingling of their movements as a whole. Fully tuned into the mesmerizing waltz happening in the space above my face, I would forget the cold and extend my arm upward as if to direct the dance. My fingers moved through the velvety light like olive oil drizzled over a fresh-from-the-oven loaf of sourdough. Slowly stirring up new choreography for the specks, I would think that I could lie here in the silence for a full morning, just watching the tiny particles do their dance in the spotlight.

I used to wonder if God was somewhere in the dust, or maybe in the light that illuminated the dust. Or maybe God was in both the light and the dust because the dance between the two was so impossibly beautiful.

Bryan still slept beside me as all this worked itself inside me and as the light moved the dust motes around me. There was warmth all over—warmth of body, warmth of mind, warmth of soul, warmth of safety, warmth of memory. The sacred simplicity of the dust that surrounded me, that was connected to me, enveloped me with holy love even when I sensed the world wouldn't always do the same.

Dust. Always there. Moving, resting, floating, twirling, dancing across the room on invisible currents even when the sun isn't around to make it known. It is ubiquitous, omnipresent even on the cloudy days when my eyes can't find it.

Dust. The dust sits thick on my memories, now brushed away as I am back in this place where my life began. The dust of me. The dust around me. The dust within me. The dust from which I came and to which I go. The presence of God everywhere in this holy gospel of dust.

3

Hobo Toast

When she was eight, my daughter Josephine and I headed across the fields early one summer morning before the sun was too high, before the day's dense heat and humidity fell upon everything with smothering effect. We were off to the farm to gather eggs, blackberries, and red raspberries for freezer jam and a fresh mixed-berry pie. She pedaled her little pink Schwinn with its detachable woven basket fixed to the handlebars down the path ahead of me while my bare feet tried to keep up. Silence hung like thick curtains in the morning air. The early dawn light was yellow and gave a lemon-vanilla glow to everything it touched. Lavender clover heads rose in the alfalfa fields like a million little Truffula trees, the gladiolus were just beginning to show some color, and wisteria vines twisted up the juniper tree along the path. There were beads of dew hanging and glistening on the ends of everything: The whole earth was decked out in diamonds, and we were underdressed for the occasion. The privilege of being surrounded by such finery never escapes me. At times it steals the breath right out of my body.

Mom and Dad had already fallen into their daily rhythms when we reached the farmyard, loading up the delivery truck for the Grand Rapids florist route. Josephine skipped toward some kittens curled up in the sunlight on a slab of stone beside the barn, the basket from her bike upside down on her head like a prairie bonnet. "Morning!" I hollered to Mom and Dad as we crossed the yard towards them. "We're here for some berries and eggs!"

My parents dropped their work to greet Josephine while I peeked in the back of the truck. So much color to see. It never gets old, the wonder of the many pigments that spring forth from the ground.

The berry shrubs stood in a line at the edge of the yard where the vegetable garden once grew. Now peonies, hydrangeas, heliopsis, a large patch of staked-up dahlias, blackberries, strawberries, raspberries, and a small overgrown vineyard of Concord grapes take this patch of ground butting up to the farmyard. While we still call this area "the garden," most of the vegetable garden has been relocated and replaced with flowers.

When my dad was a kid, his church partnered with an inner-city church in New York City. For a few days one summer, my grandparents hosted some New York City kids, those kids' first country experience. They marveled at everything—clusters of trees, creeks, flowers, plants, cows, the sound a breeze makes when it swishes over the alfalfa fields. While Gramps was taking them on a tour through the garden, he stopped, bent down, and pulled a carrot out of the ground. The kids erupted in a cackle of laughter. Amid all the giggling one boy managed to say, "I bet you can't do that trick again!"

Those words awakened my grandfather to how disconnected many are from the earth and the source of the food they eat. All he had ever known was a life where food is worked out of the ground with calloused hands. These kids believed food came from the store instead of the ground. Given the concrete barrier between them and the earth, their belief made sense. It won't be that way for Josephine. She would come to know the forty acres of ground that I and my father and my father's father knew intimately. She would come to know the source of her food and experience earth's abundance. She would bear witness to the fact that if we care for the earth, it will care for us.

As we headed to the garden, I tripped over a brick poking up out of the soil. An old rusty burn barrel once stood there, atop a layer of bricks where the yard and garden met.

Trash burning day was a thrilling event when I was a kid. Once a week or so, long before weekly trash pickup existed for those of us who lived "out in the sticks," we would burn anything that had a chance of disintegrating at the touch of flame.

We had a large rusted metal barrel, with several holes punched in the side to feed oxygen to the flames as they licked and hissed and spit. Burning trash was one chore we didn't drag our feet about doing. Often, we called our cousins from across the street to join us, and they would call us for their burn day. We became experts, generally needing only one match to kick off the party. Gathering around the heat, we started with flimsy paper and moved toward thicker cardboard, strategically stacking the trash in order to get a spectacular show of flame. Plastic packaging and Styrofoam cups were saved for last. Occasionally an aerosol can would be tossed in the barrel as we ran for cover, waiting for the thrill of a small explosion.

Plastic trash was the real treasure, though, and we stuck it on the end of long sticks, wholly mesmerized as the flame melted and warped it into odd and otherworldly shapes. The trick was keeping the plastic stuck on the end at just the right height above the fire and for just the right amount of time, preventing the thick glowing globs from melting too fast and dripping into the hot flames, where they would pop and slide out of reach deep in the barrel. One always knew how to distinguish whether a neighbor was burning trash or an old brush pile because the burn barrel smoke almost always rose to the sky thick and black. Piles of dried brush, on the other hand, sent up plumes of lighter gray smoke.

Knowing now what I didn't understand then—that burning plastic poisons the air and contributes to a warming world—my hand instinctively moves to my heart. Remorse. Lament. A brief moment of silence for the harm we caused.

Sometimes we would crack off thick dried weed stalks, light the ends on fire, pinch it between our fingers, and curl our hands around it while standing tall and sure around the barrel, "smoking" them. It wasn't a physically pleasant experience, sucking unfiltered wild weed smoke into our lungs and choking it back out, but we all played along as if it was. It was as close as we could come to being 007 or Sonny Crockett out there in the country.

As I think about it, we might have been a little bit pyro back in the day. Fires were free, fun, and filled in the gaps of our boredom. Fires pulled us into their magical warmth and mystical power. When I was in kindergarten, a couple of cousins from next door were over. Our boredom gave birth to a fabulous idea: We could build a fire and roast slices of bread on the end of sticks. We called it "hobo toast." We piled up an enormous mound of dry hay and paper from the trash. A great way to build a quick fire, yes. But where should we build it?

Trouble came because we chose the hay barn. On the wood floor. Surrounded by 150-year-old dry wood walls held together with dried out hand-hewn pine beams. Our brilliance wasn't fully formed yet, apparently.

When our pile of hay and paper was substantial enough, I ran into the house to grab a loaf of bread and matches from the cupboard. My cousin struck a match, squealing with enthusiasm over our great homemade toast experiment. In no time our fire was a roaring, raging beast. We stood breathless with our bread dangling off the end of 8-foot-long green willow branches, and our pride was stoked the higher the flames jumped. This brilliant idea was ours alone, and I was shining inside about it. We had thought of it ourselves and executed it all on our own, without any help from the adults or older brothers and cousins who usually took charge of such things.

While we were caught up in the joy of our accomplishment, Mom was cleaning upstairs and happened to glance out the window at the sight of smoke rising out of the doors and windows of the barn in billowing masses. In a flurry of panic, she ran down the steps, out the door, across the yard, and pulled us out of the barn before hauling buckets of water and beating down flames, instructing us to stretch the garden hoses across the yard.

After the flames were doused, we came face to face with our own stupidity. Everything in me fizzled out like air leaving a balloon. Our great hobo toast experiment was over. Shame moved in, replacing my pride. Mom was angry. Mom never got angry. Maybe more shaken than angry, really. Her hands and cheeks were smudged with charcoal gray, and damp hair stuck to her forehead in clumps. She ordered my cousins to go straight home and me to go inside and stay there until Dad got back.

When Dad returned, Mom sank into his shoulder and shook with sobs. I assumed her sobs were anger, but as a mother myself now, I believe they were relief. Dad would deliver my punishment. We sat on the edge of Mom and Dad's bed and his voice broke as he talked about how dangerous what I did was, and how it could have ended so badly for my cousins and me. I was to be grounded for the first time. Grounded. This amounted to no TV time and not seeing my cousins for a full week. It would be true summer torture. Dad said it was important for me to stop everything for a few days, consider what I had done, and learn to think through the consequences of what I do every day after that.

Being grounded proved to be a real struggle. A couple of days later, I snuck a conversation in with my cousin at church (groundings did not include staying home from Sunday services), and asked her to sneak over and meet me on Monday in the forsythia hedges that lined the edge of our yard. Playing with my cousins on Sunday was against God's rules and I knew I couldn't fool God's all-seeing eye, but maybe on a Monday I could pull one over on my parents. I was desperate for some relief and as long as my parents didn't know they wouldn't be disappointed in me.

All went according to plan, and my cousin and I spent a couple hours playing with our miniature Smurf figurines in the cavity inside the shrubs on Monday afternoon. I occasionally ran inside the house to grab snacks, then slinked back, stealthy as a spy, disappearing in the cavity behind the bent over branches. I discovered being grounded could be fun after all.

That evening I stood in the kitchen while Mom peeled cucumbers and sliced tomatoes. "Mom," I announced, "I'm sorry about the fire. It was really stupid, but we just wanted some toast and thought it was a really great idea—like something they would have done in old-fashioned times. I can see why you were upset, and you did a good job grounding me. You can ground me more often if you think I need it." Her eyebrows turned up and little creases of confusion formed between her eyes.

Not five seconds later, my older brother, who was well acquainted with groundings and spankings, walked in and piped up with a grin, "I can see why you like being grounded—I saw you sneaking around in the bushes with our cousin today!" No doubt he took some satisfaction in reporting the naughtiness of his goody-goody little sister.

Mom's quizzical look immediately transformed into a knowing one. "Well," she said directly to me, "since you like being grounded so much, I guess you can be grounded for an extra three days." My stomach dropped with shame and embarrassment. I hated disappointing her. That was twice in four days. The first time I didn't know I was doing anything wrong, my intentions were good. But this time I was directly disobeying her and I knew it was wrong but did it anyway.

It was like a pitchfork had been punched into my devilish schemes. Getting grounded didn't ruin the fun; disappointing my parents ruined it. I hated disappointing them.

I winced a little as I recalled all the things we tossed in that burn barrel before environmentalism entered our consciousness. But Josephine's laughter and stuffed cheeks moved my mind back to the present. Back to filling my basket with berries. Back to the garden. Back to home. Back to the place where all that was left of the burn barrel days were remnants of its brick foundation.

We finished filling our buckets with raspberries and blackberries, having popped almost as many in our mouths in the process. I looked down at Jo's springy blonde curls and berry-stained fingers, lips, and T-shirt. I was thrilled to see her with bits of the earth smudged on her smiling face. I promised to teach her how to preserve all this good food the way my mom taught me and her mom taught her.

We harvested and preserved everything growing up. We canned peaches, pears, cherries, applesauce, plums, and pickles, and lined basement shelves with them. Jams and vegetables were frozen and stacked in chest freezers. Squash and potatoes were stored in the underground storm shelter. In winter, we made fruit leather from fruit that had been pureed and frozen in repurposed milk jugs. Dad would pour a thin layer of the thick saucy juice into a large pan that sat atop the woodburning stove. My brothers and I ripped off so many small pieces of the fruit leather during the drying process ("testing" if it was ready) that there was usually only a little left by the time Dad decided it was ready to come off the stove.

Dad and Mom also made jerky from beef and venison, folding the paper-thin slices of meat that had been soaked in spices and liquid smoke over long strings. The aroma of smokiness, garlic, onion, and black pepper rolling off the meat was as difficult to resist as the fruit leather, and we often found ourselves tearing little pieces off when no one was looking. They also made large slabs of dried beef that we sliced up for sandwiches and snacking. These were salted and smoked in the smokehouse, an 8-by-8 shed with a low roof that stands beneath a cluster of pear trees at the edge of the garden.

On our way out of the garden, Josephine and I passed the smokehouse and made our way to the forsythia hedge. I parted the branches to reveal the secret cavity, suggesting she could find similar secret spaces to play in all over the back forty just as I did when I was her age. Before we headed down the path toward home, we stopped in the barn to gather some eggs.

The familiar creak whined from the hinges as I pulled open the wooden barn door. Another smell from my childhood enveloped me: a mixture of old hay, dusty stacks of boards, tractor grease, stale manure, cattle birth, and the peculiar odor of the barn's thick wood floorboards that have been smoothed down to waxiness, worn by generations of comings and goings of horses and humans and farm equipment.

Josephine headed straight to the back of the barn, where rows of chicken boxes lined a large nesting room behind a wire screen. Most of the hens had already exited the barn and were out scavenging around the yard for breakfast. A couple were still roosting inside. Josephine gently picked up a strawberry blonde hen, held it close, and stroked her back. "Good morning, little buddy." She planted a kiss on her tiny cheek. My kids adored the chickens in a way I never did when I was their age. For Josephine, every breathing thing was a potential pet. She once caught a little minnow at the pond, named him "Jimmy Junior," and took him home in an attempt to re-home him in a fish bowl filled with tap water. The cat promptly stuck a paw into the water and killed it. Josephine then filled a clay pot with soil, buried Jimmy Junior in it, gave him a gravestone, and transplanted a small clover beside the grave. The pot rested on the nightstand beside her bed for at least a year, during which time a whole graveyard, complete with headstones, slowly emerged until they had to start being buried on top of each other like an overcrowded European cemetery.

The morning light came in through long slits between the weathered barn boards, stretching its fingers across the thick floorboards, lighting up the dust that floated in the air. The mesmerizing quality of the vivid stripes of velvet light and suede darkness filled me with warmth. Josephine was busy gathering eggs. I was gathering up the past in bits and pieces.

With the memory of hobo toast fresh in my mind, I crossed a circle of scorched floorboards just inside the door. I gazed up at the hand-hewn pine rafters that have been holding the whole magnificent structure together for more than a century. Different levels of rafters crossed the barn, some thirty or so feet from the ground, and others fifteen to twenty feet high. As kids we used to lean old wooden ladders against them, and then climb up and walk across the rafters with our arms held out, pretending to be Olympic gymnasts. The older boys played ball tag, running across the narrow beams while whipping balls at each other. Sometimes we would pile loose hay up in giant mounds on the floor and flip off the rafters into them, daring each other to jump from a higher level up.

I scanned where Josephine was emerging with a dozen eggs and wondered if Mom and Dad knew, in addition to the hobo toast incident, the full extent of the dangerous she- nanigans of our childhood. I'm sure they didn't, because I can't imagine letting my kids do the things we did. It's pretty miraculous we all lived to be adults.

There were a couple of milk cows in the side stalls when I was a kid. We always had an abundance of fresh milk and fresh cream, and little else as delicious as all that. Our barn cats got fat off the excess. Dad enjoyed learning the process of making cheeses, yogurt, butter, and ice cream. The image of him sitting on a worn wooden stool, bent beside the cow, comes to me. The rhythm of milk being squeezed from the thick pink teats and spurting in quick succession into the metal pail is another sound that has stayed with me. The pitch of the milk hitting the bucket changed the fuller the bucket got, so I knew when it was almost a full pail with- out even cranking my neck to look. I loved sitting beside Dad as he worked with his quick strong hands. There's little else like the aroma of warm milk and sweet cow breath all mingled together. Sometimes, just to get a rise out of me, Dad would shoot hot milk straight into his mouth. "Want some?" he would ask.

"No way. Warm milk is gross," I would say before taking my leave.

Josephine was halfway out the barn door calling, "Let's go, Mom!" over her shoulder. This is my deep desire: to resurrect some (but not all) of my childhood experiences in the lives of my children and encourage simple living without simplistic thinking. I turned away from my past and moved through the door beside her, where the heat of the day was already beginning to gather.

4

Farmer's Market

I have been selling flowers at the Holland Farmer's Market since my dad started growing them. At age eleven, I would sit with Gramps in our aluminum lawn chairs behind an old Samsonite vinyl-topped card table. Buckets of gladiolus surrounded us in the middle of the parking lot at the civic center. Gramps always set up a big umbrella to keep a little shade on us, and we would continually adjust it as the sun worked its way across the sky.

During slow hours, Gramps would talk about growing up on the South Dakota prairie, surviving the Great Depression and the Dust Bowl. He would tell about hitchhiking to visit Grandma when they were dating, and getting lost in blizzards between home and school. He'd weave together stories about hunting rabbits and prairie dogs, and then tell the dramatic story about how he stopped to help a neighbor fix a broken wagon wheel, which led to the loss of one of his eyes, which resulted in the installation of a shiny glass eyeball. I had heard these stories a hundred times. They never bored me, and I frequently requested specific ones.

My grandmother told stories too, across the kitchen table over milk and her date-filled cookies. Grams would fill my ears with gritty details of the Dust Bowl, and how the sand pasted to her scalp, stuck in her teeth, found its way to her bed, crunched inside every bite of food, and formed a thick, filthy skin on the surface of the water in the well. Years later, when dementia set in, I would tell those stories back to her.

These days, the farmer's market features large permanent canopies lining a closed off section of street, with electrical outlets for each vendor to keep things cool in refrigerated trucks. Live music and food trucks offer a delightful array of sounds and smells. There are almost more vendors than a person can see in a single visit, and the waiting list to get a booth is years long. We were in the early farmer's market days before it was trendy, before there was a constant flow of crowds.

Gramps and I spent every Wednesday and Saturday sizzling on our asphalt island, praying our flowers wouldn't wilt in the hot sun and praying we'd sell out before we wilted, too. Gramps sat at the table in his straw hat, working his homemade wooden money box, while I stood out front, working the customers. He kept a meticulous record of how much we were taking in, scratching a tally mark in his little notepad for every bunch sold, and noting any cash we took out to spend on an apple or a quart of plums when we had a hankering for a snack. If someone was eyeing our goods from a distance, Gramps would tap my leg with his cane cut from a diamond willow tree, quietly nudging me to go "work them in."

Grandma packed sandwiches for our lunch on market days. Processed cheese slices and thick slabs of bologna on buttered wheat bread. I ate my sandwich in slow bites, savoring it. We washed it down with a thermos of lemonade, Gramps drinking from the thermos cap, me from a Styrofoam cup. Later in the afternoon, I always visited the booth of a farmer I affectionately called the "Pickle Man." He sold a variety of vegetables, but also had a large glass jar of old-fashioned brined dill pickles. Fifty cents per pickle. Gramps would hand me two quarters and say, "Go on and get your pickle now." The Pickle Man always fished out the biggest pickle in the jar for me and slid it into a plastic baggie.

One particularly hot humid Saturday, my stomach began to lurch, twisting in knots. I wanted to lie down to ease the awful cramping, but lying down wasn't an option, so I found excuses to sit between customers. I feared I might be getting a stomach bug and could possibly lose my breakfast out one end of my body or the other. I imagined the stench it would create, bubbling and cooking on the blacktop, and felt even more nauseous.

Late that morning, I asked Gramps to take care of the customers while I ran inside to use the bathroom. Dashing across the lot, I disappeared through the civic center doors and ducked into the bathroom stall to do my business. As I slid down my panties, a sticky crimson mess met my eyes. It looked like something out of a horror movie.

My first period. I panicked. I could hardly breathe in the hot airless bathroom. I had known this day would come. But why did it have to come on *this* day?!? Why on a farmer's market day? Why now? I wasn't ready for things to change, wasn't ready for the discomfort of womanhood. Why now, here with Gramps!? On a day when everything already felt so unbearably sticky?! Inhaling air that was roasting in our lungs?!?

I soaked up as much blood as I could with toilet paper. A little spot had bled through my turquoise cotton shorts. Embarrassed, I balled up as large a wad of toilet paper as I could squeeze into my panties, praying it would be enough to get me through the day, or at least to my next bathroom break. As I washed my hands, crimson water swirled down the drain. I caught my reflection in the mirror. Gazing into my hazel eyes, now forest green to reflect my mood, I hated who was looking back at me. "Suck it up, girl," I told myself, "You're a woman now." I hung my head instead.

I walk-waddled back to Gramps, securing the wad in my panties with stealth. "Things are picking up again," he remarked, "better get back up front."

I maneuvered my way forward, positioning myself between two buckets of gladiolus—one in front and one behind me. I crossed my legs awkwardly, afraid someone would see the little spot of blood. "Christy Rae, are you trying to play hide-and-seek with the customers?" Gramps was laughing.

"Yup! Playing hard to get, a new way to reel them in!" I responded, forcing a laugh back. I wasn't laughing inside. I was screaming. Crying. I just wanted this day to be over.

My clothes were damp with sweat, and the hair at the edge of my face was matted to my skin. I sat down beside Gramps during a lull. He fished out two quarters from the money box and held them out to me. "Go on and get your pickle now!" He pulled out his little notepad and wrote, .50 - pickle - Christy. A visit to the Pickle Man would be a small relief in the midst of a tragic day.

I held open my hand for the two quarters and made my way toward his booth.

"Looks like the hot week has really popped open the flowers!" Mark called out as I passed his booth. Mark sold maple syrup, maple sugar, and maple candy on Saturdays. "Do you think you'll be able to sell out?"

"No idea," I called back. "Hope so."

Things were slow and only a few straggling customers milled around the market, touching carrots, smelling peaches, taking their sweet time before heading back to their air-conditioned cars. All eyes of the vendors were on the few folks wandering through the heat. Vendors called out to me as I passed; some threw up their hands in a wave, others did the Midwest nod-of-the-head greeting. We were a small, tight little community.

Then it happened. I was waving back to someone, calling out a greeting, and I felt something slip through my shorts mid-stride. My wadded-up toilet paper skidded down and fell, like a pile of bloody bandages in the middle of the empty market. With a streak of red down the length of my leg and a face to match the color, I continued on past the Pickle Man and headed straight for the bathroom. I could hardly hold back the tears.

What a mess. I was already awkward at that age—and aware of my awkwardness. I often felt out of place and had to dig hard into my limited self-confidence to get by in the world. And now this. I sat on the toilet. Urine, blood, and tears all dripped and swirled into the bowl together. *Why can't I just stay a kid forever? Why do I have to become a woman? Why does everything have to change?!* I washed myself as best as I could, lumped a clean wad of toilet paper in my panties, threw cool water on my face, and paused in front of the mirror to take a deep breath before heading back to Gramps, this time on the back side of the vendors, avoiding the main drag and the eyes of everyone.

Gramps didn't ask me where my pickle was. He didn't ask me why I was gone so long. He also didn't nudge me up front with his cane again that day. I think he knew.

I look back now, smiling at the horror I felt but also loving the safety net under me. Gramps and Grams. The Pickle Man and Mark, the maple syrup vendor. I suppose every generation looks back at their youth with fondness, but when we left D.C., it was exactly this kind of innocent world I wanted for my children.

Is it possible to have a safe, loving community without prejudice and insularity? I hope so.

Pause, Wash, Rinse, Drain

Growing up in an old farmhouse with limited kitchen upgrades, I used to question my mom and dad's sanity in their choice to not install a dishwasher. I always attributed it to their frugal living, a lifestyle Dad picked up from his parents, who lived through the Great Depression and the Dust Bowl on the plains and prairies of South Dakota. My grandparents likely would have seen a dishwasher as a reckless splurge of extravagant spending, though their frugality didn't prevent them from eventually installing an indoor bathroom in order to ditch chilly nighttime visits to the outhouse.

Between my parents, me, and my three growing brothers who put down several meals between meals any given day, it seemed an unnecessary extra chore for my mom to have to conquer the messy stacks of dishes scattered haphazardly in piles across the counters. She rarely asked us kids to do the washing, which I always thought peculiar, though I never complained about not having such a responsibility. But why not assign the culprits of a disheveled kitchen the task of cleaning it up?

When we moved into the little house on the corner of the farm that my grandparents had built, there still was also no dishwasher. After having a dishwasher in D.C., I was expecting having to hand wash the dishes at the end of each day to be a frustrating bother. But unexpectedly, after the noise and energy of my four children subsides each night, after the juggling of the day's many schedules, after running here and there and to the moon and back, I find myself beginning to anticipate my sweet silent serenity at the end of the day in the company of dirty dishes bathing in a sink brimming with hot, sudsy water. Even better, the sink is at the base of a window overlooking the tall pine tree where cardinals and blue jays sit chatting, all fat from the seeds in the feeder, and the alfalfa field beyond that, and the woods beyond that.

In the liquid warmth swirling through my washcloth, the lilting splash of the faucet rinsing the suds, and the movement from rinse to dry rack, I am soothed. Unwound. Almost tranquilized. It forces me to pause, to ruminate over the events of the day, to be still. The sequential rhythm invites movement of the day's gathered prayers from nebulous sentiment to thoughtful, tangible release. *God, forgive me for my impatience today ... God, I bless you for providing outdoor space for my children to run unhindered ... God, give me courage to live into your way ... God, thank you for the gift of sunshine sifting through the trees and finding its way to this window.* On and on the mingled prayers disentangle, line up, and move to heaven from my heart through the cleansing of these dishes.

This act has become a point of connectedness I experience with the women of the generations that came before me. They, too, faithfully washed, rinsed, and laid to dry the dishes at the end of each long day. As I currently live in the house my grandparents lived in, a deeper nostalgia overwhelms me. I know my grandmother was bent over with the same daily task in this very sink, looking out this very window, across the stillness of this same field and forest. With all the changes from one generation to the next, dishwashing has been a constant in my family. An unbroken chain of daily routine. A task whose worth I have recently come to understand and appreciate in the context of a busy life.

A few years ago, my parents did some kitchen remodeling on their farmhouse. Among other modern upgrades, they installed a dishwasher. My first thought was, *Why now?* Their kids were all grown and all but one was out of the house. Their life had slowed a bit. They no longer faced the constant overcrowded kitchen counters, nor their rambunctious kids swarming the house with clutter, noise, and spirited energy. Now they actually have the time to do the dishes, and have fewer dishes to do.

A new reality has emerged, though, as I've begun to reflect on my need to wash the dishes. The busy days, the crazy days, the days when I'm most at my wits end, *these* are the days I especially need the space to pause, to wash, to rinse, and drain. And with it go my prayers. With the dishes, my soul, too, seems cleansed.

The seasons of life when I most *lack* the time for pause are also the seasons that I most *need* to pause. The necessary chore of doing dishes forces me to take that time when I otherwise might not.

A couple of years after moving into our little house, we began a kitchen remodel. The big question circulated around whether or not to install a dishwasher. All four kids were teenagers by then and my three boys were putting down meals between meals just as my brothers once did. If ever there was to be a dishwasher, this was the time to do it. So we did.

In the beginning, it was a fun piece of equipment to operate. Convenient, for sure. Three years later a hose got clogged and I started washing by hand again until we had time to do a deep clean of the machine. I found myself in no rush to do the maintenance. I was grateful to be doing dishes by hand again. Grateful for the rhythm. Grateful for the mandatory slowing down time inserted into my daily schedule. The dishwasher has since been repaired but still hasn't been used.

Someday my life might slow down a bit, and in a season similar to the one my mother is now in, I may be ready for the convenience of running the dishwasher again. But in this season—a season of juggling the needs of family and work and constant activity—I'll celebrate the mandatory space carved out just for me at the end of each day to pause, wash, rinse, and drain.

6

Left to Their Own Devices

I forced my eyes open after a restless night. It was 6 a.m., and my four kids were awake and arguing in the other room. Fighting a headache, I was unprepared to face the cacophony outside my bedroom door. It was only the second week of summer break.

Bryan and I had always enforced time limits on electronic device usage. At first it was twenty minutes a day, and eventually, as they grew older, an hour a day. "Your brains are still soft and being formed," I would tell them. "And even though there are marvelous things to create and learn on the internet, I don't want your heads hardwired to electronic devices. You have to trust me that I do this because I love you." Even so, they were certain I was being cruel and unfair.

Eventually they started sneaking the iPad when no one was looking. I began hiding it. They always seemed to find it. I upped my game and began hiding it in ridiculous places like in the bottom of a box of Christmas tree trimmings stored in the basement. Still (!) it would somehow be found, which always led to more tears. "It's not fair! He had it an extra hour hiding in the closet! I should get another hour too!"

I wanted to turn back time and raise my kids in the days of horse-drawn carriages and reading by candlelight. The days my grandparents invited my imagination into with their stories of growing up on the South Dakota prairie.

At my wits' end, I tucked the iPad between the mattresses of my bed, determined it would stay there all summer. But here I was at 6 a.m. hearing them snarl in the other room over a device they couldn't possibly have. I dragged myself to the living room and my jaw promptly fell to the floor. "Unbelievable." Someone had managed to wrestle the iPad out from between the mattresses Bryan and I had been sleeping on!

Enough was enough. My kids clearly had an electronic device addiction. Up until now, with the exception of an occasional spat, my kids had always gotten along well. They genuinely enjoyed being together ... until this device came into our lives.

I took one look at the scene in my living room and with a firm, expressionless face reached out an open hand without a word. My son reluctantly handed over the device. I stepped outside, dropped the device in the backseat of our car, went back into the house, unhooked the TV, dropped it in the trunk, and drove away—morning hair, morning breath, and in my pajamas, I didn't care. I was a mom on a mission.

I returned home to four shocked stares. "When I was a kid," I said, "I was allowed one hour of TV a day. We didn't have iPads or computers or video games. We had to make our own fun. Even though I didn't always realize it at the time, the greatest gift my parents gave me was the sweet gift of boredom. And because I love you all so much, I'm giving you the same marvelous gift. Merry Christmas and happy birthday." With that, I popped an ibuprofen and curled back into bed for another hour of sleep, hoping to ease the pounding in my head.

But let's be real. They were not pleased with my gift. They didn't find it sweet. There was sorrow and screeching and squirming. It was painful. Pitiful. At moments, intolerable. Punishing for all of us. Nevertheless, in my determination, I persisted through the groans, the protesting, the wailing, and the whining. I barely even flinched. I wanted my family back, and I was convinced it would be okay once they got through a period of detox.

After four days, when it was clear that I was dead serious about how our summer would look, the friendships between my kids began to be reestablished. (If they were telling this story, they would say they initially came together through their shared suffering.) Slowly, contentment started to settle into their bones as they discovered they could create experiences out of nothing and that doing so offered surprising satisfaction.

They created stuff. They read through piles of books. They constructed a village in our big sandbox complete with its own currency, economy, ecosystem, government, and infrastructure, and they each had responsibilities to keep it running smoothly. They wrote stories and made board games. They planted a vegetable garden, watered it, weeded it, coaxed it into growing, harvested it, and prepared it for the table. They scooped fistfuls of clay from the edges of the pond and built a functioning clay oven in which they would cook the fish they caught. They wandered the back forty with no plans other than to climb trees, skip stones, and become familiar with the native plants they shared the land with. Their home was outside more than in; they ran around barefoot, splashed in muddy ditches, swam in the back pond, caught frogs, fished for supper, and built small fires to fry their fish over.

Our family had never felt more connected, more present and engaged, more together, more creative, more whole than we did during the summer of 2016. It launched a life-style of intermittent mandatory screen fasting. At the end of every day the kids smelled like dirt, sweat, and sunshine. And every night they sank their exhausted little bodies into bed, eager to start over again the next day. I slept soundly again, too.

What is lost as this generation grows up in a tech-saturated world? What is friendship when it means sitting side-by-side looking at a screen while you are virtually someplace else? I am uncomfortable with how much being virtually connected is taking away from actual connection—connection with each other and with the earth. What's worse, the age of social media has allowed us to congregate in virtual silos that exacerbate rifts between us.

And yet, I am writing this on a computer. I am no Luddite, but finding the balance between the beneficial uses of technology and uses that waste precious time, diminish brain cells, and put walls between people and the natural world is a challenge. Something important is getting lost amid our technological "advancements."

I am not advocating for turning all our screens off. I use the internet for recipes and home improvement how-to videos.

I belong to a few niche groups on social media focused on things like ultra-light backpacking, Scottish folklore, bird watching, fiddling techniques, stone hunting, and other areas of interest. I have met people online who have become friends in the real world. Technology can bring us closer together, connecting us to old classmates and distant relatives, new ideas, and to realities in the world we otherwise might not be aware of.

Are the benefits worth the risks? I think about this question almost daily as I struggle to find balance in my life and in the lives of my children. Perhaps a generation or two from now the answer will come into sharper focus. Yet I wonder. If by then kids no longer know how to spend an hour in the sandbox shaping worlds with their hands, or no longer take joy in planting seeds, or no longer know how to identify butterflies by the patterns on their wings or birds by their songs, or no longer desire to settle in the crook of a tree branch with a good novel, or no longer know how to climb a tree at all, then the answer might be a devastating "no." It will not have been worth it.

My kids aren't kids anymore. As each of my four teenagers leaves home, I'll send them off with a prayer, hoping they never forget the gift of the screenless summers when they were left to their own devices.

7

The Summer of Mabel

I'm not entirely sure when the fear took root. As a kid I practically lived outdoors, going inside only to grab a book, a flashlight, or food when something fresh wasn't available from the garden or dangling all fat and ripe on a tree. Occasionally, I even slept under the stars. My scrawny little knock-kneed body, topped with a puff of untamable brown hair, was always barefoot and smudged with dirt.

We had barn cats. These were not house cats. Barn cats were wild and roamed free. I wanted to be like them. The truth is, if I'd been given a choice, I would have chosen to be a non-domesticated barn child.

I spent time on my stomach outdoors with a magnifying glass I had won as a prize at a classmate's birthday party. I spent hours making a thorough study of various insects, intrigued by their societies as I imagined scenarios for their lives. Ants were particularly interesting as they went about their busy schedules with such intense purpose, carrying insect eggs and plant fragments into their holes. I loved to drop breadcrumbs around an ant hole and then wait for them to gather and watch them take the bread into their underground bunker.

I spent hours catching crayfish, tadpoles, snakes, and frogs at the pond. Of all the creepy-crawly things, only spiders put me in a dizzy spell. There was no part of me that was curious about arachnids. No part of me wanted to study them or seek out their admirable qualities. The spider webs I encountered were immediately swiped away with sticks. If I came upon a spider, I would stamp its life out instead of learn from it. All the rest of the critters in my world were my friends. Spiders were the enemy.

It was late summer, the time of year when garden spiders began spinning their webs between flower beds. They seemed especially fond of the zinnias, tansies, and phlox. Garden spiders, though harmless to humans, are particularly vicious looking. Their large black and yellow bodies and long thick legs are the stuff of nightmares.

Arachnophobia. I don't use the term lightly. My arachnophobia got so bad I began sleeping with a softball bat. Human intruders were not my concern—we didn't even lock our doors at night. The bat was for spiders. By the time I went away to college, I still checked the dorm room ceiling and walls for spiders every night before bed.

Daddy longlegs didn't bother me. No, it was fat bodies and fast legs that frightened the dickens out of me. I was never a dainty, high-pitched, lady-like screamer, I was a yeller. And yell I did when I encountered a spider invading my space inside the house. Dad told me once, after I ran from my room in a full-throttled yell, begging him to kill a spider, that spiders took up residence in messy spaces because they liked having piles of clothes and things to hide in. I kept my room tidy from that day forward.

I was cutting zinnias with Mom one morning my first summer back in West Michigan. It was early enough that dew still clung to everything. The morning damp was particularly helpful for avoiding spider webs because it illuminated the silk strands. We encountered a web anchored between red and orange zinnia stalks. The spider was tucked under a leaf where one of her web ends was fixed to the flower stem.

I froze on the path and tensed up, reminded that we were entering the season when the webs and their weavers were likely scattered all around. "What a beautiful web," Mom said thoughtfully. Her words caught me off guard and she saw so on my face. "Oh, are you still afraid of spiders after all these years?"

"Well, I guess. I don't know. I mean, I haven't really been around many spiders in recent years."

"They're really good for the flowers, you know. Catching the grasshoppers and other bugs that chew up the petals."

I stood still and examined the web, slowly inching closer, beginning to wish I had my little pocket magnifying glass in hand. I had to admit the weaving job was stellar. Some really fine work. Intricate. Symmetrical, with evenly spaced strands of silk. The silk was lined with a slew of fat dew drops, which looked like strands of pearls beautifully adorning a regal woman's neck. In the center was a stunning section of silk with a distinct zigzag pattern, much like the pattern on a quilt my grandmother once crocheted. The middle was so thick it looked like it could be used to patch up a hole in a fine silk shirt. I scarcely dared breathe lest I disrupt the artistry. It was astounding actually. How had I missed this? I had only seen spider webs as frightening little death traps which signaled a spider was waiting to pounce. In the absence of my magnifying glass, I dug into my pocket for my phone and snapped a quick picture so I could admire it more closely when my work was done.

The next morning was drier, and our eyes had to seek out the web, lest we stick a hand in it and incur the wrath of the garden spider. We spotted her sitting in the middle of her web, waiting. I looked more closely. In addition to the intricate details of her web, she had a maze of detail across her body. She had all the markings of a monarch butterfly, but in black and yellow instead of black and orange. How had I never noticed the beauty, talent, and goodness of a garden spider?

We affectionately named this spider "Mabel" and always left the flowers uncut that she depended on to anchor her web. One morning we stopped our work and watched her move on a grasshopper that had hopped in for a meal of zinnias and gotten tangled in her web. Mabel slid across and began rolling the grasshopper like a sausage, wrapping it up tightly in silk strands to be eaten later.

I turned to the National Wildlife Federation website to feed my growing curiosity and learned Mabel is an orb spider, meaning she spins a round web. While most spiders have two claws on each foot, the garden spider has three, which are necessary for the intricate, complex webs they spin. Garden spiders are extraordinarily intelligent arachnids, and it's believed that the thick white zigzag in the center of the web is meant to alert birds, to prevent them from flying through the web and tearing it apart.

Near the end of summer, we realized Mabel had laid eggs under a zinnia leaf where her web was attached. A silky sac hung there, fat with hundreds of tiny eggs inside. I had not been aware she was expecting. I leaned in close. "Mabel," I whispered with tenderness, "you're going to be a mama."

On the farm, the first hard frost always signals the end of the growing season. When it arrived that year, I went out to check on Mabel, curious about how she handled the freezing temperatures. She was gone. Disappeared. Nowhere to be found. I assumed she went into the ground to hibernate until spring.

The website said something different. A peculiar and unexpected grief fell upon me when I learned that Mabel had begun the process of dying. It turns out female garden spiders devote their short lives to the sole purpose of producing eggs. Throughout the process, to the delight of the gardener, they eat an enormous number of insects. Her eggs would lie dormant until spring, and she would never have the opportunity to witness her little ones emerging. She was born, devoted her whole life to the next generation, and then died.

The selflessness and sacredness of her short life impressed something upon me. I began to reflect on how deeply I had demonized spiders. How horrified and disgusted I had been by the mere thought of one being near me. They were alien, monstrous, other. But when I stopped to get to know Mabel, to call her by name, when I moved in closer, read about her, studied her skills, and learned to appreciate the ways she made my job easier, it changed everything. Her willingness to sacrifice was astounding. She was no monster. She was a saint. And she had things to teach me.

I'm often reminded of the summer of Mabel as I'm bent over tending to my garden, keeping an eye out for her descendants. And I often recall her when I'm engaging with the world—particularly as vitriolic, slanderous, hateful rhetoric becomes the new normal in our toxically divided nation. We're living in times where our neighbors are treated as enemies because of the partisan label they identify with, where we have forgotten the gift that diverse perspectives are to the health and well-being of society, where the tables of dialogue, decision making, and compromise have been dismantled and repurposed into fortified and armed walls. We are quick to attach labels like "enemy" to those who bring a different perspective without knowing who they are or how they have come to their perspectives.

We have forgotten the importance of getting close to the *other*, of looking them in the eyes and calling them by name. We fail to hear their stories, fail to have compassion on those whose lives are different from ours. We cloister ourselves into echo chambers of partisan narratives that reverberate a thousand different ways. Some are brainwashed to madness and physical violence, others to verbal violence, and others to silent compliance. Few dare to speak against the extreme rhetoric and behavior in their own political party: The social ramifications are more than our deteriorated moral spines can bear. Self-preservation has risen to take precedence over communal flourishing.

If only we would sit and witness the stunning saints of the garden. If only we would be still and pay attention to what the earth is teaching us. My summer with Mabel revealed how we should behave in the world. As I exit my garden, I'm reminded that the "other" is also my brother, my sister, and like Mabel, in surprising ways, may be both my teacher and collaborator.

8

The Secret Garden

When I was pregnant with Henry, our first child, Bryan started reading to him every evening. We hoped somehow the rhythms of Dr. Seuss would penetrate the amniotic fluid and sound like home to our baby. Bryan didn't stop reading after the baby was born and more children followed. Eventually, though, our oldest children aged out of having their dad read to them, leaving Josephine, our youngest, and me to build a new practice of nightly reading. One of the books we read first was *The Secret Garden* by Frances Hodgson Burnett.

Although it was winter, my green thumb awakened and twitched as I imagined a secluded outdoor space of living walls and twisting vines, away from the world. Dreams of a secret garden began to take up space in my head and I made up my mind that although our house was small, a secret garden could serve as a lovely outdoor expansion of our living space.

Once the idea took up residency, it kept growing. One miserably humid summer night, when the window fans were only blasting hot air into the bedrooms and sleep wouldn't come and take me away from the misery, I imagined walking into a backyard secret garden. The place was so vivid and real; I knew I needed to get what I imagined on paper. I quietly lifted myself out of bed, filled a tall glass with cold water, and slipped into the bench behind the kitchen table with a pencil and my sketchbook.

I envisioned four areas: a living room with casual furniture, an intimate space for wine and cheese beneath a pergola wrapped in concord grapevines, a small room with a few garden beds containing some often-used herbs and veggies, and a large center room with a firepit for gatherings with family and friends. The walls would be hedges while the doorways would be arbors with dreamy roses, clematis, and wisteria dripping color and crawling all over.

When Josephine emerged from her bedroom with fisted hands rubbing the sleep from her eyes, she joined me at the table and I showed her my idea, whispering my secret garden dreams. In hushed morning tones she suggested a few changes. I grabbed a measuring tape and the two of us stepped barefoot out into the dewy morning. Everything needed to be measured precisely so I would know how many hedges to order for our walls.

An hour later Bryan roused, and I had hot coffee ready, along with peanut butter on toast. I remained patient while the coffee did its magic, knowing it was fruitless to share my grand backyard vision before his body and mind were fully awake. Eventually I laid the paper on his lap. "Okay. I was up last night sketching out this grand plan for how we can add space to our house, but not in our house. And without the expense of building an addition."

He looked up at me over the rim of his second cup of coffee. "Now what?" was written in his eyes. He's been on the receiving end of my many plans and big ideas throughout our marriage. He looked the plan over. "I don't really know what this is. Can't really picture it." He handed my paper back to me, somewhat annoyed by my enthusiasm so early in the morning.

"Well, I have a vision," I said. "You have to trust me. I know what this can be, and I know it will be amazing. It will be a lot of work to pull together, but not a lot of money. It will require patience because it will take time to become the thing it will eventually be. So you really have to just trust me with the plan."

"I guess it's fine with me," he said. "You seem to know what you're doing."

I ran to the farm and asked Dad if I could borrow his wholesale plant catalogs. "Yep," he said. "They're on a stack next to the couch in the living room."

"I'm going to plant a secret garden in the backyard."

He gave me a questioning look. "Okay. Uh-huh." I imagined his eyes rolling as I turned and ran inside. He had lived a lifetime of my "ideas." No doubt he probably assumed I would be planting a little circle of roses, putting a chair in the center, and calling it a secret garden. He had no idea.

After a morning looking through catalogs, I landed on the northern privet hedge to act as the walls between garden rooms. It would be affordable—especially so in a bare root wholesale bulk order. With small 6- to 12-inch-high shrubs, I knew it would be a few years before my vision would come alive, but I had to start somewhere, and on my budget I had to start small. For less than a hundred dollars, I ordered one hundred hedges and headed home to mark the placement of the walls with precision.

A couple of weeks later my shrubs arrived. When I say "shrubs," I'm referring to bare root shrubs. A small bag of one hundred short, leafless, dormant twigs with a few small roots on each one. I spent a day getting them in the ground precisely along the lines Josephine and I had measured and marked, being sure the doorways were correctly placed. Standing back after hours of sweat-inducing work, I took a deep breath and admired what I had accomplished. It was pathetic. There was nothing to see. I decided to line the shrubs with bright fluorescent ribbon, lest someone step on them or mow them over without knowing.

When Bryan stepped outside to check my progress, he had no words. He didn't understand what he was looking at. I waved my arms in a grand gesture as I revealed the living room, dining room, firepit room, and herb-garden room. This was merely the foundation, I explained. The full experience was a few years away. With flamboyance, I described how incredible it would be when the "walls" rose twenty feet and thickened up.

"Trust me," I said. "I have a plan here."

"Okay," he finally managed to say.

Determined to grow this thing, and determined to prove my vision a good one, I watered the shrubs every day, hoping to high heaven something would sprout. One day, all at once, tiny green buds popped up and down every tiny pathetic twig. Sunshine and water were doing their magic. By the end of the summer, the hedge was one to two feet tall.

Everyone in my family still doubted, except Josephine. She was excited. She believed.

Over the next few years, the shrubs continued to rise higher and higher. They fattened up and filled out and I regularly sheared off the sides to keep a straight wall and eventually began trimming off the tops after they hit twelve feet in height. Our secret garden had come to fruition like something straight out of a British landscape. My family began talking as if it had always been their idea and they had been supportive and encouraging all along.

As the fourth summer wore on, I strung up lights around the perimeter and put pea gravel down for the floors. Used outdoor furniture filled the rooms. The grapevines grew and covered the dining area with plump clusters, and we dubbed this room "France," as in, "Let's invite some friends to join us for wine and cheese in France!" In the middle of the large center room, we built a firepit out of repurposed landscaping blocks. We built couches for the living room from wooden pallets I'd pulled out of dumpsters or found alongside the road. My oldest son and I built a large arbor with two benches facing each other in the shade of the wisteria vines. Trellises dripping with clematis and climbing roses acted as doorways. My herb garden smelled of rosemary, mint, lavender, chamomile, and sage. It was everything I had imagined it would and could be.

We began spending more time in the rooms of our secret garden than in our house. There seemed to always be friends and family gathered in the garden. We relaxed out there, read our books out there, prayed out there, laughed out there, sought silence out there. Life suddenly contained a generous amount of wine and roses. We were living like Europeans in the middle of rural West Michigan.

The secret garden became a space for communal lament over what we were witnessing all across the country and in our local community as partisan vitriol was intensifying. It became a space for people to come and dream of a better world together. It became a space for group meditation and contemplation and planning actionable ways to elevate truth, to promote love and respect, to advocate for justice and peace. People in our community were drawn to the secret garden and inspired there to plant seeds of love and joy within the sadness of the world.

9

Seed Pods and Beach Stones

Over the past few years of pandemic and polarization, as
the ugliness of the world swelled around me in disappointing waves, my secret garden expanded. My need to create
beauty, to nurture life-giving things out of the ground, to see
abundance rise from seeds the size of pinheads, is the best
manifestation of hope I can envision. I cling to it, praying
that as tiny seeds of goodness are scattered and sown, some
will take root and communities will flourish in the midst of
chaos. And so I decided to make an addition to my secret
garden by creating an enormous room filled with vegetable
beds in whimsical patterns with a meditation platform in
the center.

"Are you sure you want that much garden!?" Bryan half
asked and half exclaimed. "That's going to be a LOT of work
to maintain."

"Work? Nonsense," I responded matter-of-factly.
"Working our piece of ground, making it sing with flowers
for the bees, butterflies, and hummingbirds, is a therapeutic

act of worship. Coaxing food from the ground is a liturgy that brings me joy." This is true ... most of the time. Sometimes when weeds swell out of the soil there's grumbling under my breath—especially when the heat and humidity rise higher than a steeple.

In my eagerness, I filled my seed trays early in the season, labeled them in my best penmanship, and laid them out like a well-ordered army in the greenhouse. Talk of a late Michigan frost meant keeping them in the seed plugs longer than I wanted, longer than they should have been. Their roots began butting up against confining walls, which prevented them from stretching into the deeper and more diverse soil they needed to grow fully.

Held back from their potential, I feared their growth would be stunted.

I had planted them in seed trays to begin with because seeds planted in trays in a controlled environment have a higher chance of making it from seed to seedling.

Seeds planted in the ground after the last frost might flourish, but they have a greater chance of being damaged by various factors around them. Jesus pointed all this out in the parable of the sower. Birds sometimes pluck them out of the dirt. One hard rain can wash away the topsoil and the seeds with it, while a hot sun has the potential to roast exposed seeds, frying the life out of them.

The safe space of a seed tray is beneficial.

Until it isn't.

Seedlings that never leave the tight confines of the seed tray rarely reach their potential. Their leaves shrivel in on themselves and their fruit shows up small and mangled, if it ever comes to bear at all. Roots ball and snarl around each other—gnawing and clawing, fighting among themselves for whatever nutrients they can find in the small space they are stuck in. Eventually, they will die.

My tomatoes were getting too close for comfort in their little seed plugs. I carefully and lovingly bent over the seedlings, transplanting each one into a larger container in the greenhouse to give them additional space to grow while we waited for the threat of frost to pass.

In addition to plants, I have a passion for beach stones. Some might classify it as more of an addiction than a passion. (Apologies if you're one of the people who has helped us move over the years, but think how much stronger you are today because of all those boxes labeled "stones.")

I especially love simple smooth stones. Smooth stones relax me. Their weight and shape are a comfort in the hand. That smooth calm settles with ease into my flesh, infusing perfect peace deep into my bones. We have a lot of stones lying around—on windowsills, on my desk, on the counter, on shelves, on tables, in candy dishes, in the garden. They're everywhere. I frequently hold them. Admire them. Gratefully accept the peace they offer.

Stones take millions of years to be pressed and formed. Those that roll around in lakes and rivers and oceans get their sharp edges ground and smoothed down and eventually, if I'm lucky, wash up on some beach I happen to be meandering down. Such a long arduous journey for these tiny wonders I've plucked from the sand and tucked inside my pocket.

Stones teach me patience.

Stones remind me of process.

There was a time in my life when all I wanted to find was the official Michigan state stone, the elusive Petoskey stone—a petrified coral that existed millions of years ago in only a few small areas across the world. And find them I did. The longer I chased after them the more expertly trained my eyes became at spotting them. We were traveling around the Leelanau Peninsula in Northern Michigan one summer and my husband finally said, "We have enough Petoskey stones now, don't you think? It would be nice to leave the rest for other people to find and move on to hunt for something else."

It was an idea worth considering. But what would I do on a Leelanau beach if I wasn't hunting for Petoskey stones? I had no idea. I sat on the shore with these thoughts moving through my head. Lake Michigan licked my toes with her cool wet tongue as I ran my hands over the stones scattered around me to see what other interesting things I could find. Beach glass was interesting. Then I uncovered a small agate. Those are pretty. There were lovely striped stones and smooth round stones in a variety of solid colors: black, white, red, green. Plain and simple. They were gorgeous. I picked up a chain coral fossil and studied its intricacies. Amazing. I found a couple Charlevoix stones, too. And then there were stones that resembled the color and texture of Brach's caramels. There were so many gorgeous little treasures rolling around I was a little disappointed that I had missed them for so long, having only trained my eyes to see and search for Petoskey stones.

My stone world opened wide, and I decided to follow this new curiosity and see where it led. I learned that while walking the beach, the brain and eyes have a difficult time searching for more than one specific type of stone. I had to decide if I was looking for beach glass, or agates, or the caramels. One kind at a time, not all kinds at once.

In order to really see the abundance at my feet, I had to sit down and make a thorough study of all that had washed up on shore. It required curiosity. It took a little bit of work and time to pause and dig and sift through one small pile of stones to see and appreciate the variety.

Looking back, I see how my faith had been so much like my tomato plants, stuck in the plugs too long, with an inability to grow to its potential. I stayed in place long enough to feel the tangle of roots beginning to squeeze in, blinding my vision, choking out my purpose—worse, binding up the power of God in my life, tying God's hands. God was only allowed to move in my world by the rules and interpretations of the one tiny seed pod I was confined to. There were frequent struggles among the roots in my container that sapped my time, life, and energy. This made God small.

The rules in my seed pod were shaped by a very particular way of reading the Bible in a very particular culture, built by a very particular set of doctrines written by very particular people in very particular times, responding to very particular historical events. My particular seed plug was only one out of thousands that had each developed as a result of their own unique circumstances, one out of thousands of ways of understanding and defining the mystery of the Divine. My tiny container provided one pair of dim glasses through which I read and understood the Bible.

For me, it was beneficial to be in the seed pod. Until it wasn't.

Like my long habit of hunting only for Petoskey stones while ignoring the richness scattered at my feet, I had been searching the depths and layers and piles of wisdom in the Bible only looking for affirmation of the singular narrative I already believed to be true. I didn't have eyes to see the richness outside a singular way of understanding. I was trained to see "other" as bad. What was acceptable and "good" in my container lacked curiosity. It feared discovering something different, something more beautiful and more expansive. It feared the humility that could come if curiosity led to the discovery that perhaps I had been wrong about something. The Holy Spirit was only allowed to move in the narrow confines of my seed pod.

One of my vocations over the last decade has been nurturing civil political dialogue among people of faith. I've led workshops and seminars and spoken in a variety of contexts about how to model Christ-like attitudes and behaviors as we address complex, controversial topics. One of the life-giving shifts I encourage people to make is to move away from *toxic tribalism* toward *communal belonging*.

Both toxic tribalism and communal belonging meet an important need by providing a sense of belonging and purpose. However, there is a significant difference between them. Toxic tribalism requires an enemy. It craves a sense of rightness and it needs to demonize, dismiss, and condemn anyone who doesn't get in line with the beliefs of the tribe. People who actively participate in toxic tribalism experience a hit of dopamine in the brain, which acts as a kind of high and can have addictive qualities, leading to even deeper toxicity.

Within toxic tribalism, those who are the loudest in their condemnation of others tend to be the most rewarded and celebrated within their tribe (also more dopamine!). Those who question the tribe are punished—typically shut down into submission by experiencing a loss of power, having privileges removed, or perhaps by being kicked out altogether.

Communal belonging, in contrast, doesn't view everyone who isn't in precise alignment as the enemy. It expects questions. It embodies curiosity and fosters a willingness to exchange ideas. It acknowledges nuance and complexity and is hospitable. It knows that no group of humans has ever had everything exactly right, so there is care about what sorts of words are used because those words can hurt people.

There are differing views of God as well. Communal belonging acknowledges both the vastness of God and humanity's inability to precisely pin God down in formulations and theologies. It acknowledges how deep and wide and mysterious is the love and mercy of God—beyond anything we can imagine or comprehend. It errs on the side of embodying that love and mercy as a reflection of who God is, as Jesus himself taught and demonstrated.

Communal belonging requires deep inner humility (not false public humility), something that does not come easy and requires constant nurture. Toxic tribalism, on the other hand, is so certain of itself it will harm others in the name of God.

Staying in the seed tray too long led me to toxic tribalism. The roots of my faith had become stunted, my world view small, tight, and certain of itself. I read the Bible looking for one thing—affirmation of what I had been told was true in my small seed tray, affirmation of what I already believed was the truth. I was willing to condemn and dismiss anyone who didn't see and understand as my tribe did. I felt wholly righteous and justified in doing so, because I was defending God.

I had lost the gospel plot and was doing harm to God's precious created ones in God's name.

I grew up in a tribe where, for the most part, everyone looked like me, thought like me, believed like me, and saw the world like me. I was certain my tribe had the truest understanding of everything, truer than anyone else ever had. Looking back, it's easy to see now how absurd, egocentric, and un-Christ-like my attitude was. God's image-bearers exist everywhere. They are beautiful and broken and precious and beloved, same as me. I only needed to open my eyes, sit where the water licks and laps at my toes, and sift my fingers through God's abundance and beauty to see it.

Every morning I rise with the sun, head to the quiet kitchen, put a pot of water on, and gently touch each of the rocks on the windowsill over the kitchen sink. I bless them for the many long and varied journeys they've taken toward being the unique beauties they have become. I'm grateful for the peace, the curiosity, the wonder, and the sense of calm they bring me. Then I head out to the garden with a steaming cup of coffee for some silence and meditation. Looking out over my plants, I call them by their names and consider how best to care for each one that day. And I wonder, could it all be that simple?

10

Caretakers and Pollinators

The more pain the world brings upon itself, the more I have found myself desperate to cultivate beauty. This need drove me back to the secret garden to expand its walls, to increase this haven of peace as the world raged in recklessness. I could only think to get on my knees and plant seeds that might bring beauty to a world increasingly desperate for it. I added another room for additional vegetable beds. More food. More healthy sustenance. More goodness sprouting from the earth.

January 6, 2021. The division across our country hit a new level of insanity. Extremists ransacked the place I had once worked, the Capitol, in an attempt to overturn a democratic election. How could this be happening in the United States? The fragility of the American experiment became apparent. Before long, alternative narratives emerged, challenging what seemed so apparent. This wasn't an insurrection, it was a 'peaceful protest' gone bad. Conspiracy theorists claimed deep state actors caused all the trouble. The plain truth was twisted and the future of our country—a seemingly steady, surefooted democratic republic—now hobbled on arthritic ankles and broken toes. My heart sunk as I saw many of those inside the Capitol that day waving Bibles and carrying other Christian symbols. Christian nationalism was surging, swelling in pulpits and pews of churches across the country, including here in my hometown, perverting the ancient faith.

The last-shall-be-first gospel calls us to move down the ladders of worldly power. The gospel calls us to sit with the oppressed and the silenced. It does not amplify the voices of the proud and powerful, whose bottomless stomachs never seem to reach satisfaction. The gospel extends welcome and invitation, chooses nonviolence and demonstrates love for the enemy—even at the cost of one's life. The gospel speaks truth and hates lies.

Grief began to settle into my mind and body. I had hoped justice would prevail, but politicians who had feared for their lives on January 6th soon fell into line with their party, choosing to preserve power instead of follow their consciences. In the aftermath of January 6th, I decided to counter ugliness with beauty. I added a pollinator garden room—a holy sanctuary for bees, butterflies, and hummingbirds. We forget these little ones who are critical for our own survival. We even become annoyed by them at times. I sculpted a curved walkway through the flowers with special seating in the corner to discretely watch the humming buzzing flutter of activity. What can we do but mirror what the Divine has been doing since those very first words, "Let there be ..."? Those first words began the work of shaping good things out of chaos and nothingness.

My parents demonstrated the importance of bringing beauty to the world and quietly lived in a way that brought glory to the Creator. They laid these foundations firmly in me. Dad was deeply connected to the forty acres he spent his life tending. It was always clear that this land was an extension of himself and he an extension of it. The ground was worked into him as much as he worked the ground. There was a mutually beneficial relationship between the two. They took care of each other. They knew each other. They respected each other.

When Dad wasn't working the farm, he often walked around the land in what I imagine was a kind of spiritual fellowship. Life was slow and simple with him. He walked his fields, checking on the growth of various flowers. Dad seemed to know every living thing by name—the birds, fish, trees, plants—anything scurrying about this corner of Eden. Mom and Dad walked the trails in the woods, knowing where the nests of birds and squirrels and the dens of foxes were, and spent evenings at the pond, tossing handfuls of fish food to the bluegill, bass, and catfish, and watching muskrats, geese, and ducks. Dad frequently walked his fields under the light of the moon, when a whole other group of critters were awake and busy, dashing about before the light of morning came.

The flower farm became a gracious, open-handed place for family, friends, neighbors, and even strangers who happened by. It was a place to swap stories, a place to laugh, to swim, and fish. Above all, my parents created an environment that was centered on our family. Their children and grandchildren had the privilege of working alongside each other. The farm, the land itself, became an extension of them and their love.

Mom and Dad's character was kneaded into the soil as they worked it.

Although Dad was conservative, one afternoon while we were sorting and trimming blue viburnum berries, we discussed the growing acceptance of conspiracy theories in our country and community. He was distressed by the lack of ability of people—particularly Christians—to think critically. He was upset by people's gullibility and how easily exaggerations and lies were embraced. He believed this was not only destroying democracy, but also destroying public Christian witness. He asked, "Why would anyone believe the religious truths I express if I also cling to blatant lies and swear loyalty and allegiance to the primary teller of those destructive lies?"

He feared how easily this widespread movement was spreading. He expressed concern for how it would impact the faith of his grandkids and the generations that come after them.

"Well," I said, "It could drive them away from the faith, yes. But it could also compel them into a deeper lived-out faith, one that concerns itself with truth amid a flurry of lies. It could give rise to a movement of renewal that rebels against this kind of behavior and looks inward, asking hard discerning questions of itself, too."

"Maybe so," he said, "maybe so."

I observed Dad do a small but significant thing as he tended his farm. Even though it was a weed, he preserved milkweed as best he could, saying "It's the only thing monarch caterpillars can eat. They depend on it for survival, and they're in rapid decline." He cared for the littlest and the least, and went out of his way to offer hospitality. It impressed on me more than he ever intended.

He helped me transplant milkweed from his fields to my pollinator garden. It continues to spread, creating life-giving colonies, as I hoped it would. I now find myself working around the milkweed just as he taught me—planting around it, weeding around it, and tending and protecting the new little shoots that pop up out of the soil.

I settle into a wicker chair in the corner of my pollinator garden, basking in the quiet, watching swallowtails and monarchs flutter atop the heads of purple verbena. Dozens of allium plants arch around the edge of a walkway that's lined with field stones—stones that had been tilled up by the plow and stacked in piles. There are honeybees as thick as a wool blanket hovering around the allium, Monarda, and mountain mint. Hummingbirds move with elegance up and down the honeysuckle vines, dipping their long slender forked tongues into the nectar. Random clumps of milkweed rise wildly among the lilies, crocosmia, coneflower, salvia, cosmos, yarrow, foxglove, black-eyed Susans, and hyssop.

Everything alive in this room is participating in a symbiotic communal relationship. The plants depend on the pollinators; the pollinators depend on the plants. They care for each other in a balanced way. No one takes beyond what they need. Without one, the other cannot flourish.

Oh, that the whole lopsided unbalanced world would take a turn in this seat tucked in the corner of my pollinator garden! That the whole world would come sit and see and know and understand the beauty of balance and our dependence on each other. Our need for each other in all our diversity seems so obvious when sitting still and watching the diversity interact in the natural world.

I pray that my little garden begins to radiate the kindness, generosity, hospitality, and open-handedness Mom and Dad modeled for me. I pray that like them, I may enter into a deep relationship with my small garden here and whatever other land my path might someday take me to. The sort of relationship that knows what the land needs. That knows how and when to receive its gifts, and knows how much to take, how much to tend, and how much to leave for other living things. A relationship based on love and respect.

After January 6th, I added yet another garden room—an enormous stretch of land filled with garden beds with pea gravel walkways between them. I dropped everything and put my head down as if I was a workhorse until it was finished. By the end, my bowed head had been transformed into a posture of prayer. At one end of this room, I erected a greenhouse. In the center, I created a meditation platform surrounded by lavender plants, a place for silence and contemplation as the scent of lavender fills my nostrils. I filled the garden beds with flowers and vegetables for our family, friends, and anyone in need of beauty or sustenance we happened upon.

As the world continued to brew toxic darkness, I needed to keep creating. I decided we needed to add a few chickens as well, so I built a hen house with scrap wood piled in Mom and Dad's barn. The kids and I picked out six chicks at the farm store to take home with the goal of having fresh eggs for us and whoever else needed them. When the hen house was complete, I added a front porch. The porch, perfectly positioned to look out over all my garden rooms, became my morning reading place.

Sitting there as the morning light washes the garden in pastels has become a visceral reminder of the beauty and abundance that can grow if we plant seeds and tend them with care. It's a reminder that things take time and nurture to come to fruition.

Our need for beauty, for green things, and for abundant life seems increasingly pressing. Today my mind looks ahead with plans to add another grove of trees on the back of the property. Shade for the tired. Nest for the birds. More oxygenated beauty on the earth with hopes that the world will inhale it.

The Shed

Our two-bedroom, 800-square-foot house was tight quarters for a family of six. My work was always scattered across the kitchen table, pushed over to one end in the evening when we gathered for dinner. Bryan worked at a desk squeezed into the corner of our bedroom. Stacks of books covered the bedroom floor and a maze of pathways connected the bed, the closet, his desk, and the doorway.

One night a full bladder pulled me out of sleep at 4:30 a.m.. It was always a daunting task making my way through the piles of books in the pitch of night. I gritted my teeth, hoisted myself from the edge of the bed, and carefully felt my way down the dark path. Trusting my muscle memory to get me through, I picked up speed. My toe caught hard on the edge of John Calvin's *Institutes of the Christian Religion*, knocking me off course and propelling my body forward. My face slammed into another stack of books, bruising my jaw. I winced and lifted myself from the floor as Bryan flipped on the bedside lamp. Leo Tolstoy was looking up from the floor. *The Kingdom of God is Within You.*

I cursed Calvin. I cursed Tolstoy. I cursed the invention of the printing press. I cursed our small house. I cursed myself for drinking chamomile tea too close to bedtime. I cursed the universe.

Rather than head back to bed, I went into the kitchen, put a kettle of water on the stove, sat at the table in the glow of my laptop, and began googling "ideas for backyard office space." My jaw throbbed as I held a pack of frozen peas to my face. I was done with this office-in-the-bedroom business.

By the time Bryan's alarm buzzed, my online tour had seeded an uncontainable hope inside me. I had a wonderful plan sketched out when Bryan staggered into the kitchen. As he poured a cup of coffee, I rambled on about the beautiful backyard office we were going to have. No more books in our bedroom. No more desk. No more computer. No more middle-of-the-night catastrophes. We would have a bedroom set up for sleeping, a kitchen table open for family meals, and a shed in the backyard for a designated work space. I was eager, excited.

Bryan sat down, still half asleep. "Huh?"

Once fully awake, Bryan began to share my enthusiasm, and even started doing his own poking around online. The whole process was beginning to mirror the process with our secret garden. I hoped the outcome would be as good. We decided to start by visiting some manufactured shed lots.

Most of the structures we saw seemed incapable of meeting even mediocre standards of longevity. Everything on the farm was built with solid lumber, from the house to the barn to the chicken coop. The manufactured sheds we saw were constructed of flimsy materials and looked like they would blow apart in a stout breeze. I couldn't imagine leaving our computers in any of them. What's more, my research indicated that it was less expensive to build something solid than to buy something flimsy. We just couldn't go with expensive and flimsy.

But who would build it? I knew how to swing a hammer and turn a wrench, but that was about it. Building something from scratch seemed impossible.

I began searching for used sheds for sale instead. After a few months, she appeared on my screen. Run down. Dilapidated. An ancient structure with good bones and mostly solid walls. The metal roofing looked sunken in. The windows were blown out. One side had a lean-to-like structure, and an outer wall that looked like it needed to be replaced. But her weathered wood radiated an aura of warmth and welcome. It was her asymmetrical roof line that ultimately persuaded me. She seemed straight out of *Little House on the Prairie*. She was gorgeous, and I wanted her to be mine.

I emailed the owner and made an appointment to go see the shed in a yard about fifteen miles south of us. My very skeptical husband agreed to come along.

As we pulled up the long dirt drive of the old farmhouse, the shed came into view, and I started to cry with love for her. She was even more beautiful than the pictures revealed, and I was aching to take her home, suture her wounds, and nurse her back to health and happiness. Bryan, on the other hand, lost about ninety-nine percent of the meager interest he had after he saw her. He believed she was far worse than the pictures revealed. He preferred "move-in-ready." I wanted to find a mess and make it mine.

"This is ridiculous and impossible," he stated matter-of-factly.

"I have a vision," I assured him. "I know I can fix this old beauty up."

We chatted with the owner, a local professor. She and her husband were expanding their horse farm and needed the structure off the property. It was clearly in a state of disuse and probably had been for several decades.

"It was originally a homestead house," she explained. "The farmer who lived there was going off to fight in the Civil War. His brother and sister-in-law also lived in a small home nearby. Before heading off to join the Union soldiers in battle, the brothers built a bigger farmhouse for their wives to live in while they were gone. The women raised quail, chickens, and other birds in the old house, this shed. Eventually it was home to pigs and probably a few other farm animals until it fell into disrepair."

We stepped inside. It was dark and dingy. The floor consisted of no less than a solid foot of petrified pig poop. As I had suspected, the roof, gaping with holes, would have to be replaced, and one wall needed to be replaced. The shed was approximately 20 feet by 20 feet. I wondered, given her size and condition, if it would be possible to move her.

I'll find a way, I silently assured myself.

The asking price was five hundred dollars. I estimated she was worth at least a million, so it was a really good deal. I explained to the owner that I wanted to move her, rebuild her weak parts, and use her for an office space. She raised an eyebrow. "Wait, you want to actually refurbish it? You want to use this as an office shed?!?" Her tone revealed utter bewilderment.

"Yeah," I responded confidently. "I mean, just look at that roofline." My voice trailed off into dreaminess. I could already see the shed standing in my backyard with alfalfa fields, all willowy, in the wind behind her.

"Wow. Okay. Well if you give me your word that you're actually going to rebuild this thing, you can have it for free. Everyone else who has come to check it out wants to tear it down and use the aged wood for trendy home projects. I wasn't expecting anyone to actually want to save it."

I would have gladly paid five hundred dollars, but this was even better. So much better, in fact, that I didn't bother to point out that this shed was clearly a "her" and not an "it."

"Before we seal the deal," I said, "I'd like to bring a couple construction-wise folks here to look her over. Just to be sure it can be done."

The owner agreed that this was a good idea. The next day I was back with two friends who are savvy about such things. They said it could be done. But it would be a painstaking process. The roof would have to be removed and then totally rebuilt, and we would have to take apart the walls and transport them separately on a wagon. A concrete pad would have to be poured and the walls raised with a team of people holding their heavy bulk in place while they were all reattached.

I was all in. The owner and I shook hands, and the shed was ours. As her pieces slowly began to pile up in our backyard, friends were increasingly skeptical. My dad was plowing in the field when the last piece arrived and was being unloaded. He dismounted the tractor and walked across the yard. "It's finally going to happen," I stated with enthusiasm tinting the color of my voice. I showed him the picture of her before we tore her down to remind him of what was coming.

He flashed a doubtful side eye. "Okay. Uh-huh." It was probably a polite way of not laughing.

"Dad, I have a vision. You have to trust my vision. This is going to be amazing."

I had no idea what I had signed up for. No idea this would be a two-year process of painstaking work requiring many hours of organized group help. Two years of more toe stubs and cursing during the night. Two years of intermittent thoughts of pouring gasoline on her, cremating her, and yielding to the voices that told me I had bit off more than I could chew. Two years of bending progress around seasons and weather and available volunteers. Two years swinging back and forth between hope and throwing my hands in the air.

Still, through those long two years, I refused to let go of my vision. This had to work. I needed her. And she needed me.

And then it happened. The day arrived. The final nail went in. She was standing in my backyard with all her beautiful lines intact. She was stunning. She was marvelous. She was mine. My cursing turned to dancing. Bryan swept me off my feet and carried me across the threshold. We slowly filled her with second-hand furniture and covered one wall with floor to ceiling bookshelves. Every last tightly wound bit of stress in me unwound as I carried stacks of books from our bedroom floor and organized them on the new shelves. Calvin and Tolstoy found proper homes and no would no longer terrorize me from the bedroom floor.

Bryan had an office, I had writing space, and one half of the shed was set up for group conversations and meetings. The vision and dream of what this once decrepit structure could be had come to fruition.

We didn't know that in time the shed would serve so much more than our original purposes. She became a place to gather with friends, to play games with family, to have one-on-one conversations, to do pastoral counseling, to host church leadership meetings, book clubs, meditation groups, and youth group. We didn't know that a pandemic was on the horizon and we would be broadcasting church services from the shed. We didn't know it would become headquarters for a congressional campaign.

There is something to be said for sticking on the path toward a clear vision, for persistently working at putting flesh on a dream. An idea had come in the night. After falling painfully on my face, I knew what I needed to do. I'm so glad I followed through.

12

Wedding Tree

Dad and I usually meet in the fields between my house and the farm. We find each other close to the earth, where we communicate around our shared passion for trees, plants, and birds. Regardless of our political and theological differences, we work side by side in the fields, sometimes cutting the whimsical fluorescent-colored crested celosia or the giant pastel puffs of hydrangeas. Other times we walk down the trails in the woods, noting the magnificence of the trillium as it gathers in clumps across the forest floor, lifting their delicate white heads above the mayapple leaves.

Close to the ground, we rise above the cultural chaos that is swirling around us. Connected to the earth, we remember the image of God in each other as we plant dahlia bulbs, cut fallen trees into firewood, and bend over beds of tulips. When we work together toward the flourishing of the earth, toward nurturing life from the ground, we are most whole.

A creek winds through the woods and settles in a pond before continuing its way down the fields. This flow of water is a natural dividing line between fields of rotating crops. The creek continues under a bridge built from old railroad ties and empties into a roadside ditch. From there it moves toward a giant swirling pool at the end of a culvert which burrows under the road and continues through my uncle's field across the street. Eventually it empties into a large drainage ditch at the back of his farm, a place where we used to look for snapping turtles during the day and go sucker spearing at night. The drainage ditch eventually finds its way to the Holland water treatment plant before re-emerging in every tap in town.

When significant rainstorms sweep through, the creek fills and swells, pushing water in great bursts and rushing down channels sometimes too small to hold it. The water gouges out fistfuls of earth, hollowing out the sides of the creek bank in order to make more space for itself.

When I was a kid, it was easy to lose track of time while playing in the dry creek bed during the driest parts of summer. I was a great explorer of these unknown, uncharted lands—a whole wide world alive with activity in this gouged out vein cut through the back forty. Wild plum trees lined the banks of the creek, providing a green canopy through the hot summer months and offering small juicy yellow plums later in the season. Too busy living outside to bother running to the house for lunch, I would pluck as many as I could stuff into my pockets and retreat to my "dining room" at the bend in the creek. Here a large square granite boulder jutted out of the creek bed in the shade of a Chinese chestnut tree. It was an ancient stone table fit for kings and queens and me, a scrawny kid in her brother's hand-me-downs running around barefoot with a knot of wildness atop my head. I positioned smaller rocks around the table to be my chairs. Then I would lay out the yellow plums in a neat pile atop the table, on a chestnut leaf, which was my plate, and cut the plums in half with my pocketknife. Stuffing my sunburned cheeks, sweet juice dripped off my chin as I spit the pits, trying to beat my previous distance record. I was the global champ of pit-spitting in my creek bed world.

A visit to the "bath house" was necessary in order to clean myself up afterward. I walked up the creek to the pond for a dive, sending the water skeeters, whirling water bugs, and bluegill scattering.

During spring, when the creek was too full to walk around in, the plum trees resembled rows of bridesmaids with dazzling white bouquets held at the end of long, slender arms, with white blossoms twisted in their long flowing hair. The plum trees filled the air with a sweet perfume that stirred me in ways I didn't understand as a child. As an adult, I'd call that stirring desire.

When heavy May rains swept through, my brothers and I would Huck Finn it on a large thick rubber raft down the dangerous quick-moving brown water. I imagined myself a bride riding a horse down the aisle, ducking and dodging to keep from being slapped by the bouquets. Of course, I had to jump off my horse/raft before it slammed into the bridge or I would lose my head before the vows were even spoken.

On his wedding day in 1964, Dad planted a Virginia pine. It was set firmly at the edge of a barley field, beside the creek after it winds around a bend where my stone table sat. Over the years, he tended to the tree as if it were his bride, with a level of tenderness and care characteristic of the sentimental man he was.

As the years went on, the water cut deeper and deeper into the creek bank, leaving less and less ground for his wedding tree's roots to sink firmly into. Storms blew the tree over repeatedly, dropping it across the fields, exposing the roots.

With tractors, chains, ropes, and a few able-bodied helpers, Dad took on the strenuous work of hoisting it up every time it succumbed to the weather. He was unwilling to let his wedding tree stay down, regardless of how thick and tall and crooked it became, and regardless of how severe the storms damaged its limbs. Before securing it with thick cables and heavy spikes, he trimmed significant branches off so the wind, ice, and snow had less to grab hold of. One year he cut the top clear off. Removing branches also took some pressure off the work the traumatized roots had to do to supply water and nutrients to the tree. After so much trimming, the tree stood against the horizon like a 60-foot-tall bonsai tree. Or like a giant with a really bad haircut.

It's December, 2021, and we've been hit with strong winds and freezing rain. The tree has not remained on its feet. The ice caused the branches to bend, crack, and snap. The whole tree lies across the field.

There are fifty-seven rings inside the wedding tree.

Out the kitchen window, I see Dad's silhouette sitting on the trunk as it lies like a helpless child across the field. It's early in the day and the sky is still smudged with salmon and cream. I bundle up and wander through the snow to meet him, boots crunching through a thin layer of ice that has glazed the earth. As I approach, I see grief in his eyes. He's quiet. Contemplative. Sitting on her thick trunk, rubbing his gloved hand over her icy bark.

"It was a brutal storm last night," I say as I meet him there. "I wondered if she'd make it through this one."

"Yep," he says, barely above a whisper. He looks exhausted. Spent. There is a pause. "I think this will be the last time I do this. You know, the creek is getting bigger, wider as the water steals too much of the dirt it needs to anchor its roots. It's just getting too heavy, and I'm getting too old to keep hoisting it up." He looked pained, as if he were sitting on the edge of the bed holding the hand of his lifelong love as she lay in her final moments.

I leaned in beside him to help fix the chain around the neck of the tree. Later that day, my brother, my boys, and I would help raise the tree again and fix it in place with additional heavy cables. Before the branches were cleaned up, Winston, my skilled little woodworker, gathered some of the sacred severed limbs and dragged them home to dry, to eventually carve beautiful things out of them.

Would this be the last time my dad hoisted up his wedding tree? Before summer, we knew the answer.

13

Sugar Maple

I've long swooned over the sugar maple, a slow-growing hardwood with a fabulous sense of seasonal style. It's decked out in sumptuous emerald all summer and then shows off in the fall as it spins from deep banana yellow to tangerine to a shade of red so fluorescent the mind wonders if the eyes are playing tricks. Eventually they roll a red carpet out at their feet, inviting ordinary people—not just the rich and famous—to walk it. But we don't just walk this luxurious red carpet. We sit. We lie. We even roll in it. It makes us feel like royalty. It makes us feel alive.

A large group of sugar maples is so spectacular that heaven couldn't possibly exist without these trees lining its pathways. Sugar maples have a way of hanging on to their fiery leaves long after other trees have let theirs go and are often still on fire when the first snow falls, creating a stunning and surreal landscape of flaming reds against a bright white landscape.

Back in my college days, the color of these maples in autumn at Calvin College made me deliriously happy. I snapped a few pictures one afternoon before my commute home to show Dad how lovely they were.

"Let's plant some in the field along the road," I suggested, arguing that it would enhance the beauty of our country road in the fall and be a gift not just to us, but to every car that drives past for generations to come. There is a marked difference between sugar maples in a forest and sugar maples standing alone. When they're in the forest with taller trees shading them, they don't have as much color. But when they have space to spread out on their own and absorb the sun, they're brilliant. Dad liked my idea, and we took saplings from the forest and bent over with shovels and compost and set their roots firmly alongside the road. We were planting for ourselves and for the future, because sugar maples typically live between three to four hundred years.

In winter, maples bring sap from their roots up through wood pores to recharge. The longer the winter, the more sap builds up inside each tree. When warm spring days follow cold nights, sap runs down and pools inside the trunk. Pooling sap creates pressure, and an untapped tree will find a broken branch or a deep cut to relieve the pressure. Sometimes, when the conditions are just right, sap will run while the temperatures drop, creating "sapsicles"—sweet and delicious little icicles that hang from wounds in the tree.

Maple sap was discovered by indigenous people in the Great Lakes area. Legend says Chief Woksis of the Iroquois threw his tomahawk at a maple tree in the cold of winter and the next day, which was warmer, sap began running from the cut in the tree. Woksis' wife is said to have cooked meat in the sap, launching a culinary trend for the ages.

Growing up, I never minded the task of hauling buckets of sap to the two big barrels Dad had set up in the woods. One day, while pounding in spigots, Dad, who was always up for a bit of fun, showed my brother and me his childhood sport of tree bending. This involved shimmying up a tall thin sapling, sometimes twenty feet in the air, until it eventually bent over and brought us gently to the ground. Once released, the sapling would spring back to the sky. Tree bending became an easy distraction from our chores in the woods.

When the barrels were filled, they were hauled to the sugar shack, and emptied into long metal pans and heated over a wood fire. Steam rose as the sap slowly cooked down. When the liquid had reduced to a certain point, it was poured into a large pot and set to slowly boil over the stove inside the house where it could be closely monitored.

Forty gallons of sap produces one gallon of syrup. Specific cooking temperatures determined whether we would get maple syrup, maple hard candy, maple caramel, or maple sugar. We made all of the above. Spring was a season of sweetness on the farm.

Being back home has allowed me to invite my children into the maple syrup tradition. They've enthusiastically taken on some of the work, emptying buckets for Grandpa. They love watching him stoke the fires in the sugar shack, and love that distinctive sweet aroma that floats and spins off the hot liquid like a dream. They enjoy the fruit of their labor as they drizzle pancakes with syrup, fully aware of the long process that went into the making of that moment of sweetness.

In the summer of 2021, I asked Dad where to order sugar maples for my backyard. "Oh, don't pay money for them," he said with a wave of his hand. "We can dig some up in the woods, like the ones we put along the road. But we have to transplant them during dormancy in the fall, after the leaves have dropped, or in the spring, before the buds make their appearance. Their roots can only handle the trauma of relocation during dormancy, when they aren't so busy putting their energy into the show above ground."

We waited for the right moment, keeping our eyes on the weather and the behavior of the trees. The leaves hung on well into the harsh November weather and my schedule didn't align with the moment when the saplings could be moved—there was a short window between the day the leaves finally dropped and the day we were surprised with a blinding snowstorm. We would have to wait for the spring, after the snow, but before buds sprout from the branches. In Michigan, the transition from winter to spring is full of unexpected and often unwanted surprises, so I wondered if my schedule would correspond to the unpredictable spring weather.

The winter of 2021-22 proved particularly cruel. There were waves of intense ice storms and lake effect snow that shut everything down. Harsher still, Dad was diagnosed with pancreatic cancer.

Pancreatic cancer. A death sentence under nearly every set of circumstances. But his circumstances were rare and hopeful. The cancer was discovered early, during an exam for something else, and the prognosis was good. Surgery, probably no chemo. A long recovery and then on with life.

The evening before surgery was mild. I went for a walk to both lift my prayers to the sky and press them into the ground through my feet, as is my habit. While circling the far pond, I came upon Mom and Dad out for their evening walk—a final walk before his big surgery.

I joined them for a few minutes. As we entered the woods, Dad pointed out a few clusters of sugar maple saplings that would be good for transplanting. From there, I left to walk alone, knowing it would be a few months before Dad would be on his feet and able to take his evening walks with Mom. As Dad walked ahead beside rows of tall white pines, trees he had planted on the east end of the woods a few decades earlier, I snapped a photo from behind. He walked slowly and a little bent over, wrapped in the thick, worn Carhartt coat he always wore when the weather was cold.

Dad's surgery was successful. There were a few post-surgery hiccups resulting in an extended hospital stay, but he finally came home to recover in the comfort of familiarity. His superb surgeon was able to get the cancer cleanly out, and we were grateful.

During Dad's recovery, I walked across the field almost daily to visit. It was hard for him to sit still and worse, to be stuck sitting still *inside* the house. I knew he was making real progress in his recovery when, after tilting back for a few minutes in his fancy new electric recliner, he buzzed himself upright and said, "Hey, I need to take a look at my spring planting list and the seed packets I have so I can place orders for additional seeds."

"Oh, okay. Great!" Mom said, fetching everything he needed and laying it across the long dining room table. Leftover seeds from last year, wholesale seed catalogs, a planting calendar, and spreadsheets. Mom, Dad, and I sat around the table discussing all of it. There was light in Dad's eyes—he lit up when there was a flower catalog in his lap. Perhaps there was no greater medicine for him.

He had a long way to go before being fully back on his feet, walking his fields, bending in service to his plants, but he could certainly carry on with the business of planning. Because his recovery was expected to be long, he knew he would be an armchair farmer, managing the business from his recliner or from the seat of the John Deere Gator, letting the rest of us know what needed doing and keeping tabs on how things were going. I was so hopeful seeing him at the table. He was coming around.

After a couple of weeks at home, Dad was getting stronger, doing laps around the house, pushing his walker without exhaustion. I sat with him one afternoon when his energy was up. "It's time," he reminded me.

"Time for what?" I asked.

"To transplant those sugar maples." With everything going on around his recovery, it had completely slipped my mind. I was amazed it hadn't slipped his.

The day was sunny and warm with just a slight bite at the edges. Comfortably cool. The branches were still stark, and Dad was feeling well enough for a ride to show me which

trees to dig up, and to explain how best to do it. The kids
and I piled in the Gator, shovels stacked in the back, and
we headed for the woods. My brother drove Dad slowly
behind us in the Ranger with its better suspension to avoid
a bumpy ride.

Up his well-ordered paths and across the fields we went,
into the woods and down the winding trails to the place he
had in mind, beside the last bend in the creek before it empties into the pond. Here the woods were thick with sugar
maples in every stage of life.

I planned on digging up two or three trees for the backyard.
"No, no. Take a lot," he said. "Plant a small forest behind your
house." He pointed to the leafless trees he thought were the
best and directed the dig from his seat.

"No, no, not that one. It's too small. If you dig a big ball
around the root system you can start with much bigger
ones. They take so long to grow, you know. Take that one
over there," he pointed. "It already has a good start on life."
He pointed to a 20-foot-tall tree. I somewhat skeptically
trusted him, half-doubting something so big could survive a
transplant. But he was the tree guy, so we began to dig.

We gathered the large saplings, covered the roots with
compost and dirt to prevent them from drying out, and
then parted ways. Dad headed back to the farm, the kids
and I to the edge of our yard to begin planting our little
forest of sugar maples.

When all the trees were in the ground, we stood back to
admire the work. "Just think," I said, "long after Grandpa
and Grandma are gone these trees will still be here, rooted
and growing as lovely as ever. A small piece of Grandpa's

farm growing right here in our yard for us and whoever comes next."

A couple of weeks later, there were a few setbacks in Dad's recovery. He began getting weaker instead of stronger. He felt exhausted and "off," and we all sensed something wasn't right. He was admitted to the hospital, sent home with a diagnosis of dehydration, re-admitted a couple of days and many liters of water later, and sent home with the same diagnosis, despite protests that he had been drinking a lot.

On Sunday morning, April 24, sirens screamed past my house. I instinctively ran outside to where the path to the farm meets the edge of my yard. I could see emergency vehicles pull into Mom and Dad's driveway. I ran the quarter mile barefoot down the path. Dad had tried to take a few steps with his walker with Mom by his side, but lost consciousness for a moment and fell. He was taken by ambulance and admitted to the hospital for the third time in a week.

Third time's the charm, they say. And it was. They finally discovered the source of the growing exhaustion—not dehydration, but fluid building around the heart. There would be immediate relief following a procedure to drain the fluid, which was scheduled for the next morning, Monday, April 25th.

Mom and I sat beside Dad in the emergency room that Sunday evening as the doctor delivered the news. We were so relieved to finally have an answer after a week of unanswered questions. "Dad," I assured him before I left the hospital, "tomorrow morning you'll finally be relieved of all this discomfort." With a concrete solution in place, I slept soundly that night for the first time in a week.

The call came around 6 a.m. I was just waking to get the kids ready for school. Caller ID spelled out "Holland Hospital." *Maybe Dad's procedure happened early*, I thought.

It was Mom. Her voice sounded cracked. "You have to come to the hospital. I think Dad is dying," she sobbed. "They're working on him. Pick up your brother and just come right away."

I collapsed on the edge of my bed, utterly disbelieving.

Bryan, not a morning person, jolted wide awake and held me.

"Dad is dying," I managed to say. As soon as I said it, it struck me that he was *dying*, but *not dead*. I jumped up, managed to get out of my nightclothes, and wrestled my badly shaking body into whatever clothes happened to be closest. "I have to go. I have to go right away. Need to pick up Jon and get over there."

Shaking behind the wheel, I struggled to see the road through the blur of my tears. Even though my speedometer registered sixty-five, it never took this long to get into town. It seemed as if my wheels were in quicksand, and like every vehicle in front of us was out for a slow Sunday drive.

We pushed through the hospital doors and into his room, where Mom was bent over the bed wearing every shade of sadness, grief, and disbelief on her face.

Dad was already dead when Mom called. They had been trying to revive him. But now he was officially gone. His relief did finally come, but it was not the sort of relief we had hoped for. At 6:23 a.m., before they were able to do the procedure, his heart stopped. Just stopped. He was here. Then he wasn't. It was impossible to grasp that he wasn't.

Dad, tomorrow morning you'll finally be relieved of all this discomfort. I hadn't been wrong, but this was not the sort of relief I had in mind.

His body was still in his hospital bed. It didn't seem real.

Mom sat down beside him and looked so small. She wept into his weathered, tough-as-leather, green- and brown-stained hands. Hands that had defined and shaped so much of my world. Hands that served those around him. Hands that held the hymnal on Sunday mornings as he sang loudly and out of tune beside Mom with her sweet heavenly voice. Hands that spent a lifetime cultivating life and joy out of the dirt. Hands that should have still had life in them.

My other brothers arrived, and we hugged and cried and sat in silence, waiting for reality to settle in. It didn't. It wouldn't for a long time.

I stepped out of the room to call Dad's siblings. Two nurses down the hall were chatting away. My breath wedged in my throat and a flash of anger swept through me. I wanted to throw down my phone and scream at them, "Hey! My dad is dead! How dare you be happy?" Instead, I prayed, "God, make the world stop! Reverse the hours and fix it!"

As we sat with Dad's body, I continued to have difficulty registering reality. I didn't want to leave him. I wanted to will life back into him. Maybe the doctors had given up too soon or missed a faint heartbeat. The whole scene seemed to take place outside of myself, yet was also happening somewhere deep within myself.

On the drive home, movement outside my car window was exaggerated and shocking. People bustled about their business—pumping gas, entering and exiting the grocery store. Birds swooped above, gliding like tiny ballerinas floating above a stage. How dare they? An elderly man walked his collie down a sidewalk. Closer to home, farmers on tractors were churning their fields in preparation for spring planting. Unthinkable. Would spring actually have the audacity to come this year? Everything should stop. Everyone should cease moving. The world should pause for this moment and acknowledge what it had lost.

Eventually, I found my way back to the farm. His farm. The farm he grew up on, raised his children on, the farm his grandchildren were spending their summers working alongside him on, the farm he built and tended. How could we possibly exist in this place without him?

We gathered at Mom and Dad's. Bryan and our son Winston, who was his grandpa's shadow, walked over from our home. My seventeen-year-old boy bent his strong, muscular body down onto his grandma's slender shoulder and trembled with the kind of sobs I hadn't seen since he was a five-year-old. His grandpa was not coming home. How could Winston exist without his grandpa?

We went to the funeral home that afternoon. Mom and Dad had already made most of their funeral arrangements. Thank God for their foresight. The Bible passages for the funeral service had been selected, as were the casket and gravesite, and everything was paid for. As we sat with two funeral directors discussing the plans for the visitation, service, and burial, we were instructed to pick out some clothes for Dad's body and bring them back to the funeral home.

We were just about to dive into the topic of music, which Dad had not specified, when Bob from the funeral home chimed in with both pride and seriousness, "Just so you know, our embalming process is one of the best. It's pretty incredible. You could actually dig up the casket in fifty years and Howard's body will look exactly the same as it does when we bury him."

I almost lost what few bites of lunch I had managed to swallow. I was stunned. Bob's words took all the sacred out of the room.

"It's really some of the best and latest embalming available." He was smiling slightly.

"God Almighty," I silently prayed, "please strike Bob down right here so he can get a taste of his own fine embalming process. At the least, dear Lord, deliver unto him severe intestinal distress so he'll be compelled to run from this room and leave us in peace." Instead, I hesitantly nodded. I was numb.

We flipped through a hymnal, trying to decide on songs that were both meaningful to Dad and appropriate for the funeral. Classics. *Great is Thy Faithfulness* maybe. *Peace Like a River* perhaps. *My Jesus I Love Thee*—Grandma had that one at her funeral. But all I could think about was Dad, blanched and preserved like a string bean in a Ball jar, headed for storage in a concrete root cellar. Available to be opened at a later date, apparently. *What the heck, Bob. No one has plans to dig up our dad!*

Ashes to ashes and dust to dust. But, according to Bob, not really.

Modern technology allows us to lay bodies to rest pumped full of scientifically advanced preservatives, sealed in silk-lined, fine wood coffins, placed in concrete bunkers, to prevent the dead from coming into contact with the dirt of the ground. Dad would never again be with his beloved earth. I wish I hadn't heard any of those details from Bob. I suppose it was meant to be a comfort, to assure us that the thousands of dollars paid to the funeral home would result in Dad's body being treated with care. But Dad was of the earth. He didn't need to be preserved from the earth.

That afternoon, Mom and I slid the door to Dad's closet open and tried to decide what he should wear in his casket. I ran my fingers over his shirts. So many memories stitched in the fabric of his clothing. So many moments lived. The long-sleeved, brown and blue plaid cotton button-down shirt he wore when he sat atop the tractor under the blaze of sun. The suit reserved for Sundays, weddings, and funerals. The thick green shirt he wore on fall days too warm for his Carhartt coat. I wasn't sure where to begin. "I guess we first need to decide what kind of thing to dress him in," I said. "Suit? Button-down and tie? Sweater? T-shirt?"

"Definitely not a suit," Mom responded. "He was only a Sunday suit person. So, I think a casual plaid button-down makes sense for him."

I agreed, thinking to myself, *Dad doesn't need to meet Jesus in his Sunday best. He intimately communed with God out in the fields.* Then another thought came to me: He'd be more easy to spot in heaven looking like himself.

The hamper in the corner of the bedroom caught my eye, with its lid slightly open atop a bulge of dirty laundry. Dad's clothes were in there. His scent would still be on them. Mom would have to lift them out of the basket, take in the last smells of her beloved before washing, folding, and packing them away forever.

The next morning, I rose exhausted after a sleepless night. I stepped outside and threaded my way through the back forty. Up trails and down drives, across fields, through the woods, around the pond. Dad was nowhere to be found. And yet, he was everywhere.

I thought of how his sweat was stitched into the soil. I imagined his skin cells caught in the cracks of willow bark. And I saw his footprints, lodged in the soft ground in all his usual places. I begged the sky never to rain and wash them away.

I moved slowly, with my senses attuned to the work of his hands—his carefully planned and planted fields and gardens—rows of pussy willow, curly willow, red twig dogwood, holly berries, viburnum berries, hydrangeas. Patches of hellebores, peonies, gladiolus. I wanted to remember exactly the way he left things.

I stepped into his little winter sanctuary, a repurposed greenhouse inside a grove of tall white pines. His axe was lodged beside a tidy stack of firewood with his leather work gloves on top. In the corner, a small radio stood atop a log. Beside the radio, there was a kerosene heater and chair. He'd sit in the warmth of that place to take a break and quietly watch the snow fall. I sat in his chair and picked up the gloves that recently had held his thick fingers. I pressed them to my face searching for his scent, and wept.

He was just here filling this space, and then he wasn't. I stood and walked outside beneath the pine trees—so tall, straight, strong. The ground beneath them was topped with layers of slender needles. I dropped to the ground and lay on my back and drifted into a sad, dreamy sleep, waking some time later to the noise of geese on the pond. They must have flown in early this year, perhaps to offer a mournful song for the man who provided them with a safe summer home and nesting spots for their young. The whole earth was off-kilter and they knew it.

In the days that followed, I vacillated between the pain of absence and the joy of sweet memories as we went through slides of road trips, camping, and everyday farm life. My concern about how Mom would adjust accompanied my disbelief that he was actually going into the ground. He should be working the ground.

Everyone dies. I know this. But in some upside-down way, I guess I never believed my dad would actually die. He was too bright to be snuffed out, too strong to be taken down. How does one get on in the world without a dad anyway? I had no idea.

In those first days, while swirling currents of ache, goodness, gratitude, and emptiness collided inside me, my eyes fixed on the sugar maples outside my back window. They represented the last beautiful blessed memory I had of my dad.

We put his body in the ground on a Friday. He was buried in the sandy soil of our local cemetery, near the edge of a downward wooded slope, with a view of the farm through the trees.

That evening, my cousins, who grew up on the farm across the street, joined my brothers and me in the back shed for a time of remembering. We gathered in a circle, with thoughts of Dad in the center. Over scotch, we told our stories, recalling his easy ability to step away from everything when the opportunity to horse around with his kids, nieces, nephews, and grandkids presented itself. He worked hard, and he played hard, too.

We laughed and cried until after 2 a.m., at which point I dropped into bed. The emotions of the day slowly unfurled and eased me into a deep and precious holy sleep. His was a life fully lived, to its unpredictable end. Even in the midst of my grief, that somehow felt right.

Our house felt like a funeral parlor, with floral arrangements perched on every available shelf and table. The pastor said that in all his years of ministry he had never seen so many flowers at a funeral. Flowers stood like choir members in colorful robes, spread across the front of the sanctuary and curled around the coffin.

It was hard to be in the house with all those flowers, so I headed out the back door to wander. Up, down, and around rows of Dad's blossoming plum, peach, and apple trees, through his stand of pines, down rows of lilacs, beside patches of daffodils and hellebores and trillium just starting to pop across the forest floor.

The flowers in the house reminded me that he had died. But out in the fields, the flowers reminded me that he had lived. When I got back to the house, I pulled the flowers from their vases, piled them up on the counter, and marched that pile straight to my compost pile so they could decompose there. They would bring life and nourishment to next year's garden. In this moment, they reeked of death.

As I turned from the compost bins, my eyes were drawn across the yard to the sugar maples. They had sprung buds at some point during the week. They had made it. My sugar maples had survived the transplant. I took a slow stroll through them. They were going to live. They were going to grow. Those buds seemed the only appropriate forward movement of the week. I shed a few tears at their feet and was surprised by the slight smile that dared to emerge on my face. I gave an approving nod, then slowly slogged back to the house, back to the rest of my life.

14

A Perfect Pearl

It was one of those thick wintry days in the middle of a long string of thick wintry days. I was desperate for some fresh air, so I did what you do in Michigan when you are in need of fresh air during winter: I swathed my body in layers, strapped myself into my snowshoes, and headed out for a trek. In my earbuds, Itzhak Perlman was playing Johann Sebastian Bach's *Sonatas and Partitas for Solo Violin*.

The drifts had swelled to waist deep overnight, but the day was a perfect calm. Snowflakes wafted slowly down, all thick and big and buttery soft. The white of winter swallowed me. It was all around me, all over me, and under my swaddled feet. It stuck to my hat, my red snowsuit, my lashes, and I took bits of it in with every breath.

As I made my way, I imagined a satellite picking up an image of me from outer space—a tiny red ladybug, slowly moving through this giant milky landscape. I moved at a lumbering pace, but I also felt very alive while being swept up into this snow globe.

Despite the ten-degree temperature, I was warm and snug in my layers of clothing. The earth seemed snug, too. It was still and silent and my mind convinced my body that I was moving through a thick fleece of white wool. The snow that swallowed me swallowed all sound outside my earbuds, and I felt the line between reality and illusion blurring in that dreamscape.

Bach entitled his *Sonatas and Partitas for Solo Violin,* "*Sei Solo,*" which means, "You are alone." He wrote it after his first wife, Maria, died. Bach's music can be heavy and complex, with complicated rhythms and multiple musical stories going on all at once. Although a musical genius, Bach isn't alone. His style is typical of the Baroque period.

"Baroque" means "misshapen pearl" in Portuguese. Baroque harmonies are loaded with modulations and dissonances. There is harshness to the intonations and much of the music has weightiness to it, as if shackled to the wall of some damp windowless basement.

But *Sei Solo* is different from other Bach pieces and typical Baroque music. It has a long, liquid emotional line that pulls through the harshness and hard edges. There is a free-flowing tenderness, a sweetness that many of Bach's better-known compositions lack. It is pure silk, spun off the strings of the violin, and it wraps itself around my heart. Instead of being showy, it is simple and sacred, like a silent prayer offered at an altar. There is beauty inside its expression of grief and aloneness. It's not a misshapen pearl, it's a perfect pearl, in the middle of the big misshapen mess of the world.

In the quiet and the empty of the back forty on this day, Bach's brilliant composition is gravity, pulling me deep into the heat of his emotions. I continue pushing myself through the snow toward the back edge of the woods. How can such beauty and perfection arise out of so much pain and tragedy? How can such sweetness be born from the ashes of grief?

I step beyond the tree line at the back side of the woods and cut a trail through dense white to the middle of the back field. Perhaps, I think, in sadness, our need is for something good, and so we are compelled to create beauty when the world isn't giving us any.

I tried after my dad died. I made tea out of lavender from the bouquet that sat atop his casket. Tied a string around the stems and hung it upside down to dry in a dark closet. The flavor of the tea wasn't quite right, so I gathered pine needles from beneath his beloved wedding tree and added them to the boiling water.

It tasted gray on my tongue and failed to provide warm comfort to my body in the way I wanted it to.

My son Winston tried, too. That first Christmas without Dad, Winston whittled a beautiful wooden heart out of a branch Grandpa had trimmed off his wedding tree. Winston mounted the heart on a flat piece of wood and put a wooden frame around it. He wrapped it in cranberry red Christmas paper and wrote "Grandma" on the gift label. We all cried when she unwrapped the gift. A gift from my son to my mom, made with love. A gift from my dad to my mom, tended to throughout the good and bad of their fifty-seven-year marriage, reflected in the fifty-seven rings of their wedding tree. It was a reminder of Dad's love and life-long commitment to her.

The heart hangs on the wall in the living room beside Mom's reading chair.

Today, on the backside of the woods where the trail opens up to a now-hibernating alfalfa field, I am away from the world. In the middle of a square-mile country block, a hundred million snowflakes drop from the sky and look surreal against a stand of dark pines. I pause to take it all in. "You are alone," I hear Bach whisper in the spaces between the notes. I'm standing in an open field with nothing but snow for as far as I can see. There was a brief pause and then *Andante* from *Sonata No. 2, in A Minor* began. It seemed as if the timing had been orchestrated by an invisible conductor.

The beauty of this particular composition in this particular moment brought tears to my eyes. I was fully open to what it had for me. Away from the world, away from cultural expectations, away from the voices telling me who I must be and how I must behave—here, there is no holding back. Here, there is relief, release, and complete undoing. I inhale deeply and fall on my back into the snow. Into the earth that loves me. I am who I am, even if I am alone. I sense beauty and contentment in the mystery of this moment—here in this place. I am alone. But in this moment I am absolutely who I am.

Here I travel to heaven on a swooning, swooping, sweet melody even though my body never leaves the snowy ground.

The song is planted in me. It becomes a part of my history, part of my body and soul, as surely as every blood vessel, bone, and tendon, every emotion and angle of my personality is a part of me. The song grows flesh, and it is mine.

When I was a child, we had a large console containing a record player set up in the dining room of the old farmhouse. In those days, record players were also pieces of furniture. My mom had inherited a small collection of albums, and I used to lie on the dining room floor at the foot of the console listening as the music of the New York Philharmonic Orchestra cascaded over me. My eyes would trace the cracks in the patched plaster walls and transform them into entire universes spinning through space. They were playing Bach. His compositions were astounding. The music rushed over me like a river driving down a steep mountainside. Bach was almost too much for me.

We didn't have much in the way of stuff when I was a kid, so the precious few things we did have were cherished. Mom's records were among the cherished. I developed a deep fondness for the soft, crackling sound that came along with the music through the speakers. Now, as I lie here in the snowy field, the only thing missing is the crackling in the background of every song that plays through my earbuds.

There was mystery in the music from that old console. I had a deep sense of being connected to something bigger than myself. The music made me feel refined even though I wore my brother's hand-me-downs. It made me feel rich even as we scraped by. I felt part of a marvelous community that crossed oceans and spanned centuries.

In middle school, I saved up enough money to buy a state-of-the-art Panasonic stereo system that could play albums, tapes, and CDs. It could hold two cassette tapes and five CDs at a time. My friends listened to the latest pop music—the stuff that rises, then fades away—Chicago,

Tiffany, Madonna. I was drawn to classical music—the stuff not of a decade, but of centuries. I saved my hard-earned garden chores money for a five-CD classical music collection from the music store in the mall. My friends, with their little shopping bags of frosted pink lipstick and dangly earrings, rolled their eyes at my choice. But what was a pair of cheap plastic earrings compared to timeless wonder? These were things a thirteen-year-old couldn't explain to her peers. I just knew.

Five CDs for a five-CD-changing player couldn't have been better planned. It was pure joy to unwrap the tight plastic covering, slice open the seal, and send them spinning on the disc changer. The stars had aligned and now I had continuous Bach, Beethoven, Chopin, Mozart, and Tchaikovsky while I read and did my homework. It seemed that all the technological advances of humanity had been leading to this moment, for this five-CD set to be paired with this stereo system and for both of them to be in my possession. This music took me places nothing else could.

I lie in the field, an insignificant speck between earth and sky, hardly knowing where one ends and the other begins. Bach's *Andante* expands inside me, pushing through my body. An unnamable thing is unfolding and I can't believe how beautiful it is. My lips tremble as if prayers are slipping out uncontrollably at the feet of the Holy of Holies. I should maintain reverence and silence, but my body can't help itself. Even though there are no words, I am singing. Loudly. Bach is a priestly figure and his music a sacred word that rings truth throughout the ages.

The gospel according to Bach, spoken from a pulpit in this sacred sanctuary, filling my soul and inspiring me to live beauty into the brokenness of the world. To transform my own pain into something lovely.

The earth spins through space, and seasons turn. Populations die and new generations are born. Humanity expands and fills the earth. Poverty, war, drought, famine, and disease wipe away pockets of precious life. Power structures swell, are overthrown, and are replaced by others that eventually crumble, too. Fires devour forests, and saplings lift from the ashes, stretching their arms up into new forests where fires return again to lick them away. The continual rising and falling, swelling and slowing, dying and rising, climbing and coasting, ever-evolving movement of the earth and its inhabitants rolls through time, space, and history.

And there, like a steady thread of spun gold stitched straight though it all, is the music of Bach. In the world's pain, there is Bach. In loneliness, there is Bach. In hardship, there is Bach. In love and goodness and deep abiding joy, there is Bach. In the great dips, there is Bach. In the fat swells, there is Bach. Across cultures and throughout time, there is Bach. His music, a steady constant vibrating presence, a common language across continents, as the living breathing world moves in and out of chaos.

The snow rises around the sunken heat of my body, and I think about the rising and falling of my life, too. I think first about the loss of my father, and how he loved every inch of this farm. Then my thoughts widen. I reflect on all the faces and stories that have been woven in and out of my life. I think about the pain of loss, the pain that comes from being hated, despised, rejected, because of the transformative processes in my life—processes that have changed me into someone different from so many people around me, people I love but who simply don't know how to love me back. I think about the people I once demonized who are now my friends and collaborators. There is so much rising and falling, continual death and rebirth. And here I am, living my one life within one quick blink of time. It is easy to despair, but Bach reminds me that there is always hope hidden under the piles of ashes, waiting for its moment to burst through the darkness.

While everything fluctuates, Bach stays. Through the great rising and falling of time and all its windswept changes, there is Bach, a steady constant presence in the rising and falling of my life, too. As predictable and faithful as the seasons of the earth. A misshapen pearl? Not for a minute. Perhaps the harsh grinding of sand and time that claws, scratches, and scrapes around inside the oyster is precisely the thing needed to turn out a perfect pearl.

15

Sweetie

Sometimes I name the birds that take up residence in my secret garden. There always seems to be a flurry of activity, particularly in the vegetable garden room, as house wrens, blue jays, song sparrows, warblers, robins, and others sit atop the fence posts and trellises, chattering away and singing their tunes. One year I came to call a certain robin "Sweetie," as it seemed to suit her disposition.

I had watched Sweetie spend early spring gathering grasses and twigs to build a sturdy nest for her little ones. She had perched the nest atop a large wooden tomato cage near the potting shed. I regularly spied on her progress through the zoom lens of my camera and cheered her on. If bird-watching was an athletic event, I would be in the stands, obnoxiously cheering for Sweetie, waving a homemade banner, embarrassing her in front of all the other birds.

Eventually she laid a beautiful blue-green egg. And then another. Then two more. The beautiful color of robin eggs protects the embryos from harmful UV rays and from overheating in the sun. It's remarkable how cleverly designed even the smallest things upon the earth are.

Sweetie sat on those eggs day and night. She covered them during torrential downpours and in high winds and through an off-season snowfall.

One morning as I was headed out to the greenhouse to check on some seedlings, I spotted blue eggshell fragments scattered on the ground below. Little squeaks came bouncing out of the nest from beneath the belly of the mama. "Great job, Sweetie. You did it," I whispered softly, so as not to disrupt her and her newly hatched little ones. She sat there with a look of both tenderness and pride. I felt proud of her, too.

Day after day, I watched as she fussed over her growing babies. First, she fed them regurgitated food. Eventually, she began pulling worms and insects out of the compost pile and dropping them into her baby birds' eagerly open beaks. At feeding time, they looked like all beak, but the beaks were attached to their awkward and perfectly precious little bodies, now sprouting fuzz on the tops of their heads and showing signs of incoming feathers.

It was a marvel, witnessing her love and care for these little ones. All the hard work she had undertaken in preparation for their coming. The sacrifices she made. The way she willingly absorbed the harshest elements in order to spare them from the worst of it. She covered them with her wings, kept them safe and well fed.

One afternoon, I made my way through the secret garden to the pollinator garden room. Some dinnerplate dahlia bulbs had arrived, and I was eager to get them in the ground. The sun was midway through its daily course, and a comfortable seventy-degree breeze swept over everything. As I rounded the walkway to the corner of the room, I heard the distress of Sweetie in the next room over.

I had never heard her like this before. I moved down the path to the sight of her nest, her beautiful home, turned over upside down on the ground. Almost at the same moment my eye registered a cat sitting at the far end of the path that wound through the vegetable beds. He was licking his lips. "No!" I cried, running to the nest.

Three of the babies were gone. One was left splayed on the pea gravel, still alive, having fallen a short distance from where the nest had landed. I gently picked the baby up and placed it back in the nest and set the nest in its prior position. I prayed Sweetie would settle down and come and tend to this little one, who must have been traumatized.

I was angry. Aggrieved. What a waste of life! So much work and care poured into those little birds. They did nothing wrong. Just happened to be in a place where a cat was prowling about!

Sweetie was devastated. I was devastated. I began weeping alongside mama bird, somewhat surprised at how deeply all this was affecting me.

"They're just birds," I whispered in an unsuccessful attempt to console myself.

I crossed the garden and approached the cat who was looking rather proud. He was an unfeeling, uncompassionate animal who was just doing his instinctive animal thing. I knew this, upset as I was.

Two little broken bird bodies lay at odd angles on the ground near him. Lifeless. Unmoving. Just a few days short of when they would have become fledglings and flown the nest. The fourth bird was nowhere to be seen.

I picked the cat up and cried my tears into his silky fur. I knew my sobbing meant nothing to him. I knew he didn't have the capacity to understand how upset I was over the consequences of what he had done. He is an animal, after all. Human tears and heartache wouldn't be enough to make this animal understand.

I picked up the two limp little bodies. Cupping them gently, I carried them back to the pollinator room. As Sweetie continued on with her mournful wailing, perched atop a watermelon trellis in the vegetable garden room, I buried her babies in the soft soil alongside the dahlia bulbs. Their first watering was the tears that dripped off my cheeks.

It was a devastating afternoon in the secret garden. And these were just three baby robins. Just three little birds, part of a kingdom of animals.

I've made a distinction between the earth and the world, calling the earth what God has created and the world what humans have created. I've leaned in the direction the poet Gerard Manley Hopkins leans, when he calls the world "seared," "bleared," and "smeared with toil."

But what happened in the vegetable garden room was the earth, not the world. Nature. At times, heartless, cold, and cruel. There are food chains and survival of the fittest and other occurrences we'd rather not look at. But look we must if we are going to have any wisdom, knowledge, and compassion about both the earth and the world. Must we look? We must.

16

Swords Into Plowshares

When one of our cats killed Sweetie's babies, I was angry. But I wasn't angry at the cat. He was following instinctive behavior and being true to his cat nature. But when humans who know better misbehave? That sends me to my garden. I enter my garden for the tactile reminder that persistent planting, watering, weeding, pruning, tending, and coaxing can nourish a life-giving community of green things as they push out of the ground. I enter my garden to see the fruit of hard work—to know that all the bending and kneeling under the heat of summer with sweat pooling in the folds of my skin always yields good things. I enter my garden to be reminded of how the world can be if we work diligently toward a vision of its fruition.

I especially needed to be in the garden because in 2020, my husband, Bryan, a pastor, ran for the U.S. Congress. As a Democrat.

A Christian pastor ... running as a Democrat ... in West Michigan. We knew it would be a difficult experience, but we never imagined the extent of the vile things that would come from the mouths of people around us. I expected disagreement and pushback. I was not prepared for cruelty. I spent a lot of time on my knees in the garden throughout his campaign.

Politics can make people anxious. Especially people with strong relational ties, like family ties, but with differing political views. To keep the peace in those cases, politics is often a taboo subject. But politics is simply the way we decide how we're going to live together—whether in our cities and townships, our state, our country, or the whole world. Politics is important. Yet it isn't everything. My experiences in Washington, D.C. taught me that.

I mentioned in the introduction that when we left D.C., we were burnt out and decided to leave ministry. When we moved back to Michigan, we began to meet other people who'd had similar experiences with the church. In one way or another, the folks we met had given up on the church but not entirely given up on God. Eventually, we gathered these folks together for a book study—meeting in the backyard. Over time, as the group kept growing, Bryan began to feel called to start a new church in Holland. It would be a church for outcasts and rejects. The Christian Reformed Church, the church of our childhoods, was not spacious enough to hold the variety of religious views our group had. We found a home in the United Church of Christ.

The more time we spent serving in the community, the more we began to see patterns of struggle emerge as a result of systems that were broken or unjust. Our new church community had spent years petitioning our government representatives for more compassionate systems. We advocated for those who couldn't overcome obstacles despite their best efforts, believing advocacy is an appropriate aspect of our public testimony of the love of Christ.

We kept raising our voice, but it felt like we were crying in the wilderness. After years of silence and indifference from our elected officials, Bryan was asked to run for Congress.

His response, at first, was a solid *no*. But after months of conversations with folks in the district and time spent in prayer and contemplation, he eventually found himself compelled to say *yes*. He said yes knowing full well he would not and could not win. He knew from the outset a win was inconceivable in such a solidly conservative district. Bryan decided to run anyway in an effort to say some things that needed to be said and to put forth a campaign that modeled a better way of engaging in politics. His campaign would speak truth, avoid hyperbolic and slanderous rhetoric, engage issues with deep thoughtfulness, and offer creative alternatives. He would name the good in his opponent, not make extremist statements, and highlight common ground between Republicans and Democrats.

In spite of these high ideals, before the end of the tumultuous 2020 election, we were forced to move out of our house twice because of violent threats. People regularly drove by slowly, shouting obscenities before peeling off with a roar. Some in our children's Christian school community made it clear through anonymous letters, emails, and social media posts that our family was unwelcome and unwanted at "their" school. Our kids endured more than I care to write about here. Some day they may choose to tell their own hard stories, but it's not my place to do so. We were slandered in unmentionable and dehumanizing ways, including having local pastors tell us we were not real Christians, that we were acting as the devil's agents on earth. Strangers wrote monstrous, heart-stopping words about our family and boasted about the ugly things they were going to do to us, including detailing how they would have their way with me and my eleven-year-old daughter.

Q-Anon conspiracies were taking root in our community, and every absurd thing coming out of the secret and mysterious person called "Q," who sat in a dark basement somewhere crafting vile and heinous statements, began to be attached to Bryan. He was accused of being a Satan-worshipper and of supporting violent protests. He was said to hate the Constitution and hate true Christians, wanting to criminalize Christianity. A picture of Bryan and our daughter in a local park was taken and put up on social media with a caption about pedophilia. People mindlessly ate this stuff up and regurgitated it on their own social media platforms.

Why? Because there was a "D" beside Bryan's name on the ballot. That was enough to justify vilification and demonization. There seemed to be no end to the violent, poisonous rhetoric, including from many self-professed followers of Jesus.

Dehumanizing labels have always been a precursor to violence against various people groups. Always. It was stunning to realize this kind of cruelty lurked beneath so many of the polite folks we moved among on a daily basis. Was this something new or had it been there all along?

Thank God, our family also experienced strong support from many others. Turns out there were parents at the school too terrified to publicly let anyone know they were Democrats. They stood by us. So did many warm-hearted, frustrated Republicans. Without their support, we would have had a much harder time surviving. It's said you find true community in difficult times, and this proved true for us.

In the days leading up to the election, author, activist, and personal friend Shane Claiborne took a hammer to the barrel of a gun and transformed it into a garden trowel for me. This wasn't a first for Shane, he has toured the country doing a modern version of turning swords into plowshares. His inspiration is from Isaiah 2:4: "They shall beat their swords into plowshares, and their spears into pruning hooks; nation shall not lift up sword against nation, neither shall they learn war anymore." Shane turns guns into garden tools as an act of resistance to the normalization of violence. He reminds us that God's people are supposed to be planting and nurturing—not killing.

Gripping the carved wooden handle and plunging it into the soil day after day became a reminder that Christians are called to be people of life and hope in every aspect of our lives instead of death and destruction. We are called to bring light to darkness, to love instead of hate. We are called to embody God's way of shalom in the midst of a cruel and chaotic world. We are called to self-sacrifice in the service of others—not to sacrifice others in service of ourselves.

Gardening has become a contemplative practice where I've learned to examine myself and release the hatred hiding in the corners of my heart. In the silence of the garden, the Divine whispers that planting and tending leads to life, and violence begets violence. As I bend over my plants, my grief and anger are worked out. My tears mingle with the soil of the vegetable beds. (I take my anger out on weeds as I tear them from the ground.) This is holy, healing work.

In the garden, I imagine what would be possible if we had the strength and humility to beat not only our literal weapons but our partisan weapons into plowshares and work together. I imagine what could be if we cast a vision of a world where everyone had the opportunity to thrive and then threw ourselves into the work of making it so.

The campaign was grueling, but things were said that needed to be said. While it did not result in a victory, it was like a giant wooden spoon stirring the pot of our hometown and district. Many folks who identified as Christian and therefore assumed a Republican identity by virtue of West Michigan culture were poked enough to pay attention with a degree of consideration.

The campaign held "Pub Democracy" events around the district in which Republican and Democrat constituents were invited to come together—not to hear a campaign pitch, but to hear from each other about their hopes and dreams for the world. It was powerful to witness people realize we struggle under the same broken systems and desire the same kind of world. We are not enemies, and could even be powerful collaborators.

Politicians and pundits are profiting immensely off our hatred of each other, and once people see this, it is impossible to unsee. Stepping out of our overheated and angry silos, into the blue sky and the sun we forgot was overhead, many folks were inspired to lay down their partisan weapons and work side by side within their spheres of influence.

As people came together in the midst of toxic division, I felt hope. Bryan went into the campaign knowing it was a longshot he would win. He didn't. Despite the costs to our family, it was worth it. Something new began to grow in the hearts of people his campaign touched. People began to experience the power and beauty of laying down their weapons and picking up tools.

The more time I spend in the garden, the more I sense the Spirit of God hovering around and within, and the peace that passes understanding begins to take root and grow. As I experience that holy peace, I find myself able to let go of the self-pity and resentment that I had felt during the campaign. The more I experience God's peace, the easier it becomes to pray that God's Spirit would bring peace to the hearts of those who sought to harm us. The more I pray for God's peace to enter hearts, the more I believe it can be so. The more I believe it can be so, the more confidently I go about living into that hope.

As I kneaded the soil and pulled the weeds around some cabbage plants in the garden one day, a remarkable and unexpected thing began to take shape within my own heart. Dare I name it? It was compassion. Compassion for those the world tells me to hate.

May all my weapons be transformed into tools that persuade life out of the various soils I find myself in. If I am diligent, life can rise up out of the ground, even where it seems an impossibly hard soil to soften, even if that hard ground is the soil of my own heart.

17

Seasons Change

In autumn, the sky churns like a turbulent sea; disheveled yellowish clouds rimmed in dark gray gather in clumps over the landscape. Shadows stretch longer as the sun arcs lower and lower in the southern sky. The daylight hours are clipped short. Gray squirrels zip frantically across the yard burying hazelnuts, chestnuts, and black walnuts for winter stores. The quaking aspen have already shed their garments, which lie decaying across the wet grass. The trees stand naked while the glacial wind whistles around their spindly limbs.

It will be a brutal winter, according to the *Farmer's Almanac*. Out in the fields, we spend the days digging up dahlia bulbs. Our fingertips freeze as they sink into the wet clay. We burn the peony field to prevent the stalks and foliage from harboring fungus that will deform next year's growth, and we cut perennials down to stumps.

The garden has given up the last of the harvest. We can tomatoes into sauces and salsas and organize them in the pantry in tidy rows. We twist the final acorn and butternut squash off their vines, stacking them in a cold corner of the basement for winter soups and bakes. Eggplant, zucchini, green peppers, and jalapenos are pulled from their stalks before bone-chilling temps arrive and nip them with frost. Grapes are plucked and squeezed into juices and jams.

Winter is on the edge of tilting hard upon us as we finish the harvest. I brace myself for the cold and sunless Michigan months, hoping for a steady gentle snow to fall upon the earth and keep our world bright. The last of the geese have flown in formation for warm southern temperatures, leaving us without so much as an echo of their deep-throated calls lingering in the sky. I already long for their return.

We were a few months into Bryan's congressional campaign and our peaceful little country home and yard had been fitted with cameras because of violent threats. The stress was weighty enough to break my spirit some days. Sleep came in fits and starts as my brain was attuned to every noise outside the house. In the midst of this, my period failed to arrive on schedule.

As I stepped out of the shower one morning, I realized it had been a full two months since my last menstrual cycle. I wiped my hand across the steamed-up mirror above the sink. "Oh Christy, you're not just late, you're *very* late," I whispered to the woman looking back at me. "Shit," she responded with a somber look of concern.

I had gotten pregnant with two of my kids while using birth control, so I guess I shouldn't have been surprised. But

I was in my mid-forties. I *was* surprised, and not in a good way. How could I be pregnant now?

The timing was terrible. My youngest was eleven. We were done with the baby/toddler era of life and fully into the tweens and teens phase. And with the additional stress of the campaign, I wondered if my womb was even capable of nourishing another life. I was having a hard enough time taking care of my own body.

I decided not to tell Bryan. Not just yet. He was stretched thin putting in thirty hours of campaign time every week on top of his full-time job as a pastor. The nature of the campaign meant he was navigating the thorns and thistles of slander and cruelty at every turn. What he was carrying seemed too much for his quiet, calm, compassionate nature to bear. He refused to sling back the mud, carrying it with a kind of love-your-enemy grace that demonstrated the core of his character.

"Aren't you going to respond to this garbage?" I would ask in a raised voice. As I mentioned earlier, Bryan was accused of a series of outrageous things, including being a pedophile and Satan-worshipper bent on criminalizing Christianity. "They're lying about you! They keep putting words in your mouth that you never said!"

"No," he responded calmly. "You know I'm not going to play those dirty games. How will American politics get better if we don't model something better?"

He was right. His character would shine through. But it was hard to witness his good name being dragged through the mud. It physically pained me. Because of how much I felt the campaign in my body, I assumed I would probably miscarry.

I took a pregnancy test. Negative. *Must be too early*, I surmised.

Over the next two bloodless, sleepless months, I took seventeen pregnancy tests, all negative. I began to fear an even worse reality. *Cancer. I have cancer.* I began to notice symptoms. Sleeplessness, which I had attributed to stress. Weight gain, which I had attributed to pregnancy. Joint aches, to the point where I could hardly walk when I woke in the morning. Exhaustion, which I also attributed to pregnancy and stress. But now it was coming into sharper focus: cancer was definitely ripping through my body. Probably in my bones by now.

I went to see my primary care physician and sat in the examination room bracing for the worst. Near tears, I waited for the news of my impending death.

"Menopause," he said. A big word. Spoken so casually. It struck me like a plow hitting a large chunk of buried granite and the whole scene unfolded in slow motion.

"Sorry, but did you say, 'menopause'?"

"Mmhhmm," he said, scrolling through my chart on his laptop.

"So, not cancer? I'm not dying then?"

"No. You're not dying. I understand it can feel like that though."

"Um ... but ... menopause is ... well ... wouldn't you say that's an *old* people thing? I'm not really old yet."

"Old*er* women usually, yes," he affirmed, glancing at me over the wire rim of his glasses. "But it does occasionally hit younger women such as yourself."

I reminded myself of the good news: I was not pregnant and I did not have cancer. No more babies swelling inside my body. No chemotherapy. But another kind of change was afoot whether I liked it or not. And I definitely did not.

I had been so certain I was about to bring new life into the world that to discover my body had, in fact, reached a point of being unable to do so ever again was tough and strange to come to terms with. I didn't want another child, but it was upsetting to realize that the choice to do so was taken away by none other than Mother Nature herself, my bestie.

I decided to try and manage the symptoms medication-free, as they came. The earth changes without intervention, I reasoned. Seasons come and go without intervention. The trees of the field experience birth and death over and over as they surrender to whatever season falls upon them. I can do that too. I can move through this with self-awareness. Feel and embrace the changes and attune my body and my life to them. I can surrender myself to the realities of menopause and push through to the other side. This is just a part of nature, so I began reading up on supplements and herbal teas to help manage the symptoms.

Over the next year, my condition worsened. I felt like I was part of the compost pile at the edge of the garden. Deteriorating. Breaking down. Everything in my orbit seemed out of my control. Bryan began holding my hand as we fell asleep, as if to anchor me while the world outside and the world inside me spun in chaos. I could hear his hand speaking to mine through our tangled fingers. *You are not alone. I'm by your side. I've got you.*

Even so, sleep came in fits and starts. I frequently woke in a hard sweat, damp bed sheets twisted around my body. I was prone to peeling off my clothes, half awake, half asleep, heart running fast, breath heaving under scorching heat and the feeling of extra insulation around my body. I would throw the windows open, hoping the ten-degree winter air would crawl in, curl around my body, and slither down my tight throat to help me breathe again. I lay on top of the bed half-dressed, being cooked alive. Bryan lay beside me with every available blanket atop himself to prevent frostbite.

Half an hour later, I would violently slam the window shut, complaining about the freezing cold. I would grab blankets from my tortured husband with my greedy, sleep-deprived hands, burying myself until the next hot flash hit and the whole process repeated itself.

I went to bed exhausted. I woke, equally exhausted. Every. Single. Day. *They do this to people as a form of torture,* I thought, *they keep them awake.* Menopause should be legally categorized as torture. There should be commercials from lawyers offering compensation for the violations our bodies are forced to endure against their will and without just cause.

Aches and pains seeped into my joints with such relentless force I was certain I had aged thirty years in a few months. Rising from bed in the morning, my ankles and knees and hips felt as if they might crack and crumble beneath me. I held on to things to steady myself, wincing as I took slow small steps across the bedroom. I moved like a woman in a nursing home heading down a hallway. I figured I'd proba-bly need a walker by Christmas.

My clothing size climbed steadily, and the more the weight bunched and gathered around my middle, the more exhausted I became. It felt like I was carrying rocks jammed inside a backpack I could not peel off. My brain receded into a thick soupy fog and there were no lighthouses to guide me back to clarity or solid ground. My whole existence was a muddled mess.

I tried every available natural remedy and nothing eased the symptoms.

A year in, I was frazzled, depressed, strung out, exhausted, moody. At the same time, our two youngest children were entering puberty. Hormone-induced energy was thick in our small house. Then came the coronavirus pandemic, and all four kids moved to remote learning inside our 800-square-foot home. Borrowed card tables squeezed into the corners of our living room became their classrooms. At the same time, we figured out how to lead our church over the internet.

I was going mad. While I sat at home alongside my husband and kids, my eyes studied the house. I didn't like the way things were. Dark cabinets with some doors hanging by one hinge lined our tight galley kitchen. The vinyl floor was old, cheap, chipped, and peeling. The '70s burnt orange and brown shag carpet in the living room had endured my grandparents' active lives and a slew of renters after them. No doubt this carpet was caked with every kind of microbial nastiness imaginable. The walls were darkly painted paneling. The more I looked, the bleaker it became. I swear the walls actually began closing in as the pandemic went on.

I began to imagine the darkness away, replacing it with light. White paint, knocked-out walls, new floors. One day my brain found a clear passage to my hands, and I began slinging a sledgehammer into a wall and ripping out carpet. I needed to control something, and this became it. I needed brightness. I needed our house to feel like a place of light.

Bryan couldn't even form a full sentence when he walked in and saw what I was doing. "What the …?"

"Trust my vision," I assured him. "And stay out of my way. I have a plan."

"But how will you even ...?"

"YouTube," I said matter-of-factly. "It will teach me everything I need to know."

The timing was terrible. Everyone said so. I went on with my plan anyway. They'd seen this movie before, first with the secret garden and then with the backyard office shed. They knew to stand back and let me do the thing I needed to do. Besides, no one dared get in the way of a mama in menopause.

In the midst of the madness, I opened Facebook one morning and someone had posted the well-known prayer of St. Patrick. I read through it, but my brain twisted every "Christ" into "chaos."

Chaos with me,

Chaos before me,

Chaos behind me,

Chaos in me,

Chaos beneath me,

Chaos above me,

Chaos on my right,

Chaos on my left,

Chaos when I lie down,

Chaos when I sit down,

Chaos when I arise,

Chaos in the heart of every man who thinks of
me,

Chaos in the mouth of everyone who speaks of
me,

Chaos in every eye that sees me,

Chaos in every ear that hears me.

My house projects were out of control. My body was out
of control. The political rhetoric in our community was out
of control. My hormonal kids were out of control. My emotions were out of control. I needed to breathe.

As I stood in the Mexican food aisle at the local grocery
store one afternoon, a hot flash pounced on me, nearly
knocking me to the ground. It was the hottest, most hellish
one yet. My brain spun like a Tilt-A-Whirl. Unaware of my
behavior, I threw off my jacket, unbuttoned the top of my
shirt, then kicked off my shoes and peeled off my socks to
feel the cool floor on my feet. I was tempted to throw my
whole body onto the floor. Anything to extinguish the pulsing flame that burned and crawled over me. Sweat dripped as
I clenched my fists around the shopping cart and struggled
to breathe. Cans of black beans and salsa spun and blurred
around me. I felt delirious.

An older woman quickly approached, pulling her phone
out of her purse. "Are you okay?" she asked frantically. "You
might be having a heart attack! I'm going to call 911!"

I put a hand up, "No, no, no. No need to call 911," I said
between quick shallow breaths. "It's menopause. It will be
over in just a bit."

Her frantic energy softened to a knowing empathetic look. "Oh, honey. I'll stay with you until it passes. And it will pass, you know." She gently put a hand on my back as I stood gripping the grocery cart. "Not just this hot flash. But all of it. Menopause is just one uncomfortable season you have to get through to arrive at a new era of life. The *golden* era," she added with a wink. If the wink meant fun and mischief and peace and new adventures, I wanted it, and quickly.

Her words and presence brought to mind another grocery store encounter I'd had several years earlier, with another smiling elderly woman. I had been in the checkout with all four kids—all toddlers at the time—one in the seat crying, one sitting inside the cart loudly banging cans of soup together, and two hanging from the sides of the cart, upset and crying that I had said "no" to the overpriced pushup candy pops in the checkout display. I was near tears when a woman approached. She patted me on the hand and said, "You don't know it yet, but these are the best years of your life!" She similarly gave me a knowing grin and a wink before walking out the door.

What was it with old ladies giving me knowing winks in my worst moments?

Years later, I can see that she had been right. I look back to those days when our children were very young with incredible fondness. Perhaps the woman beside me now also knows what she's talking about. I stood, body on fire, clinging to her assurance that the golden era was just around the corner. She picked up my coat, socks, and shoes, and guided me to a table at the in-store Starbucks. After fetching a cup of cool water, she sat beside me and entertained me with hot flash tales—horror stories in the moment, but gut-splitting humor in retrospect. She assured me that someday I would be able to look back and laugh at today's event, too.

"Well," I said, "I hope that day comes sooner rather than later."

It did. It came three weeks later, when I finally caved and slapped a CombiPatch on my abdomen. I did what I had told myself I wouldn't do. I went pharmaceutical and the patch delivered sweet estrogen relief from the debilitating symptoms I had battled for almost two years. Out in the garden, I had harvested the provisions to nourish my family through the upcoming cold Michigan winter. But it turned out I could not endure such a hard season unfolding in my own body naturally. I needed medication, a product of the world. Life is complicated like that.

YouTube proved to be very helpful in guiding my renovation endeavors to the fruition of my vision for the house. Our cramped quarters began to feel more spacious and bright. The sunshine that filtered through the trees and flooded through the south-facing windows poured across the whole house and lifted my mood. It brought me to feel an expansion within myself as well. I was different. But I was going to be okay.

One of the earliest lessons I learned on the farm is that seasons change. How hard it can be to accept this lesson in my own life.

18

Lavender Dream

One warm summer evening I head out, barefoot, feeling the weight of the off-kilter world. A study had been released that day indicating that the climate is heating at a pace quicker than anticipated and will likely reach a point of no return in my lifetime.

We're all connected as part of the divine design. Field, stream, boreal forest, white-tailed deer, song sparrow, earthworm, soil, sand, air, human beings. There is a delicate balance between all things. But human greed, human activity, and human carelessness have upset that balance. Through drought and famine, those living in poverty are experiencing the worst of it. Extreme weather patterns are already wreaking havoc. There has always been extreme weather and catastrophes, but the frequency and intensity of these events is on the rise.

I wander out to a great open space on the back forty to confess and surrender my sadness to the clover that lifts its lavender head across the alfalfa fields. *We're in this together, you and I*, I say with my eyes as I lie down and rest my arms at my side. A simple stunning serene landscape of purple puffs gathers in clumps across an ocean of emerald. This ethereal scene is surrounded by what looks like a ballet of willow trees swishing and swooping their skirts in the breeze at the perimeters of the field.

As I settle in the grass, cloud wisps swim in the blue overhead. I lie with my hands and arms open. Ready to let go. Ready to receive. Ready to exhale hopelessness and embrace the possibilities I see everywhere upon the earth. The tiny lavender spheres bend and rise like monks before an altar. They bow in worship, and I cannot take my eyes off them. Such delicate little puffs, forces of beauty thriving in small communities with honeybees and tiger swallowtails fluttering between them.

As my eyes scan the remarkable earthscape, I feel held, cradled in the warm arms of Mother Earth. She accepts my body and receives my tears without question. She sees and knows what is happening across the surface of her own flesh. Wars tear into her. Unfettered consumption scrapes and gouges her, and then fills garbage heaps that seep poison into her. The engines of progress cough, chug, and churn without taking into account the slow killing of everything.

She preaches. The Great Reverend Mother Earth. But the world turns its ears away from her wisdom because we are too busy listening to the swell of our own puffed-up voices. Our own theories, our own doctrines, our own ideas.

"Consider the lilies of the field," a great teacher once said. But who has time for that? It would require that we sit still and keep quiet. It would necessitate that we stop clamoring and reaching and shouting and spouting and grabbing all the things we are told to want but do not need.

She shows us exactly what we need, demonstrates how we ought to live, preaches timeless truths, and dazzles with ever-unfolding mysteries. Her existence inspires deep awe and wonder.

The more distant we become from the earth, the more we view her as a thing to be exploited. The more we normalize her exploitation, the more we laugh at the wisdom she has to teach us.

I become breathless as I consider my own smallness upon the earth; my own fragile state and the temporal reality of my existence. I am just a speck, birthed out of a chance encounter between a microscopic sperm and egg, briefly pulsing with life before being whisked off in some unpredictable fashion to whatever comes next. I consider the earth: just a speck swirling around the sun. I consider the solar system: just a speck among countless other solar systems in the galaxy. Our galaxy is one of an endless number of galaxies. I feel my smallness. I am indeed dust. What can one little speck of dust do?

I recall a teacher in my Christian school having Proverbs 1:7 written on her pushpin bulletin board. "The fear of the Lord is the beginning of knowledge, but fools despise wisdom and instruction." This verse scared me. Was I afraid enough of God? Could I *know* God if I wasn't afraid? In seminary, I came to understand that the word *fear* here is more accurately translated *awe. Awe. Wonder. Awesomeness.* Unlike fear, this was a concept I could understand. Awe of the Creator was easy to feel. I experienced it often, laying under a night sky smeared with the Milky Way and a million stars piercing the darkness or gazing upon a blue sky with cotton white clouds swirling through it. Wonder came naturally as I strolled a winding path in a forest of hardwoods or stood at a pond watching water bugs whirl and dive with speed and grace.

Awe of the Lord is the beginning of knowledge, but fools despise wisdom and instruction. We are in danger of becoming fools when we fail to sit in awe and wonder of the created world.

My lifetime, whether long or short by human standards, will hardly be a millisecond in the billions of years the universe has been in motion. Human existence itself is but one whiff in the history of our planet. It's said that if the earth was formed at midnight and the present moment is the next midnight, humans have been around since 11:59:59 p.m. One second. My body trembles as I reflect on what I will do with my one little life. Will I leave my part of the earth better or worse than it was before I came to it? Will my engagement with the world contribute to wholeness? Or fracture? Will I create chaos or shalom? Will I use my millisecond to chase after riches or to join hands with others who seek to better the world? Will I lift up the low places and promote communities that love peace and pursue justice? Will I live with open hands or clenched fists? Will I walk lightly on the earth or frantically scoop out as much as I can for my pleasure? Will I leave puncture wounds that contribute to human struggle long after I'm gone?

One little life. So much potential to shape the moment it's in, for better or worse. Can I gather the earth inside myself and take it with me as I walk in the world? This earth, my source of life, light, and hope, my assurance and resting place, where I experience God's deep love and wisdom. The earth that is of me and within me settles me when the world makes me anxious. Can I maintain a closeness to Mother Earth—never forgetting her face, never forgetting what she needs, always remembering her wisdom?

The awe of the Lord is the beginning of knowledge, but fools despise wisdom and instruction.

I arch the small of my back and stretch out my arms, brushing my fingertips across the soft clover heads and consider the possibility that if the whole world would stop every now and then and lie down on some patch of ground, it could inspire enough energy to change the world. This becomes my wish for the world. This becomes my lavender dream.

I pinch off a clover blossom, run its softness over the curve of my cheek, down the bridge of my nose, and bring it to my lips, sucking the sweet nectar from its petals. Swallows swoop and dive around me as this dream swells up and begins flowing from my lips. My lavender dream is a prayer, and I hear myself singing it.

Losing all sense of time, I continue in fervent petition as the air turns smoky gold and drizzles across the western horizon. A sliver of moon is suspended in the sky as I make my way across the field in the encroaching blackness. As I move toward the lights of home, I feel full of holy, earthy aliveness. It has seeped into my skin, my bones, and my tendons. It pumps through my heart and winds its way through the neurons of my brain. It ignites and sharpens my eyes to see the realities of the world around me, to see what we are doing to the earth and its inhabitants, to know there is a better way and to work toward it. I remember that I am a part of all this too—the hard and the holy, the severe and the sacred.

Once home I pick up a pen, my music journal, and my guitar. I scratch out an evensong for the world, my petition for a path to wholeness, my simple lavender dream.

Lavender Dream

Come lie with me out in the field.
The clover's in full bloom, a bed for our wondering.
A kiss from the breeze, embraced by the sun.
Wide open ocean of lavender dreams.

Lavender dream.
Away from the world.
Close to the earth
and possibility.
Lavender dream.

Spinning through space and rivers of time.
Clouds drifting over, wafting in blues.
Drink in the deep, hushed and alive.
Inhale the fragrance of lavender dreams.

Lavender dream.
Away from the world.
Close to the earth
and possibility.
Lavender dream.

Grounded and free. Awake to the now.
So large and so small. The universe breathes.
Back in the world with eyes full of earth,
our minds will awaken to lavender dreams.

Lavender dream.
Away from the world.
Close to the earth
and possibility.
Lavender dream.

19

Rooted

When the things of this world feel sad and weighty and the skin of the earth is stretched thin and bustles with more destructive activity than it was ever designed to carry, I wander out back where green things grow. When the wisdom of the world is foolishness, the earth centers me on what is good and right and holy and wise. When life's cruelties and disappointments exhaust me, I get inside some patch of earthy aliveness, and that earthy aliveness gets inside me. I become, in every sense, rooted. Quiet wisdom is whispered from the mouth of the earth. I only have to be still enough and quiet enough to be able to hear it.

I lie in the field, and the grass lifts its long slender arms above me, catching its sleeves on the dim current of breeze. Bending and swishing. Choreographed sashaying. The curves of my body fuse and smolder into the soft curves of the earth. A familiar lover. Cumulus clouds move overhead heaped like cauliflower on a clear glass platter down a long dinner table. It's a slow familiar procession across cerulean skies. Mourning doves rhythmically lift lilting coos from their throats. Lullabies. Sweet songs from the earth. Balm for my wounds and a reminder to keep singing despite everything.

I swallow the air and let all the weather, all the seasons, all the sorrow, all the joy, all of nature's fantasia and fury beat fully upon my wide-open face. I embrace it. All of it. And it embraces me back.

Morning is my favorite time to wander, to wonder. The earth seems freshest in the early hours when the breath of night still lingers in the air and the sky is a romantic smudge of caramel and peonies. At times I'm certain it's just me and the earth in these very early hours when all things seem possible.

In spring, I walk through fields, letting the warm thick rain lick, roll, and slide down my cheeks. My bare feet squish through spongy fields with nut grass and mud sieving through my toes. Life is breaking through the hard crust of winter. Daffodils, crocus, tulips, forsythia. The orchards match the morning sky as I move down rows of apple, peach, pear, crabapple, cherry, and plum. Dogwood blooms delicate as china ripple in the breeze while heaps of lilacs make me dizzy with their scent. The earth is refreshed. All things are new. What seemed dead begins to pulse with life, rising from the ground. Everything is awakening. And I with it.

Summer burns away the heavy rains. I'm bent over the blossoms of summer. The dirt is warm under my feet. The ground pulses through my body. My back aches, legs ache, sweat runs freely, leaving streaks down my sunburned cheeks. I feel wholly unworthy of such noble and difficult work as this. Bent over, I tremble in the presence of all this majesty and miracle. At the end of the hot days my exhausted body cools off, slipping headlong through the cool satin sheets of the pond. Here, I am revived as the residue of the day washes off. And the unpleasant residue of my life seems to get washed away too.

As the oak and the sugar maples slowly fade from emerald to crimson and their leaves float downward, caught in the swell and song of autumn breezes, they eventually make a mosaic on the ground. I lie on that holy ground as it spins through space, watching the winnowing trees shed their garments around me. Light filters through colors like stained glass. My back arcs to meet the tumble of leaves and I inhale the scent of earthy decay. Inhale. Exhale. The forest sheds what is old here. And so do I.

Winter comes. Snowflakes float and tumble, intricate works of art crocheted for only a brief moment, a blessed gift for whoever happens to be paying attention. The brown edges of autumn are buried in these tiny masterpieces. The snowy field becomes an oddly warm bed to lie in as the white sky floats down around me and over me, nibbling at my cheeks with a flirtatious tenderness. The earth is soft and quieted. And I, with it.

May I learn to embody for the world all that the earth has embodied for me.

Here I am rooted.

Here, where my roots stretch into the earth. Here, where the earth's roots stretch into me.

Home.

Acknowledgments

It's hard to string together the words to adequately express my gratitude for all the people who came alongside me in the process of telling this story.

I am deeply grateful to my parents, for the way they loved and nurtured me, and for the way they loved and nurtured the land. They have modeled love, hospitality, and generosity with the whole of their lives—with all that they possess and all that they are.

This book would not have been possible without the support of my family and their unwavering encouragement throughout this process. Special thanks to my husband, Bryan, for cooking dinner and plowing through stacks of laundry and dirty dishes when I was working my way through heaps of words, phrases, and paragraphs. Gratitude also to my four kiddos—Henry, Winston, Charles, and Josephine—for always reminding me of what's important, for surrounding me with joy and delight, and keeping my feet on the ground. Your presence steadied me.

For the land itself I give thanks. For the forty acres that fashioned me—for bluegill that swirl the surface of the pond as it reflects the setting sun across its surface, for oak and sugar maples rising in clusters above mayapples, and trillium that carpet the forest floor. For rolling hills whose valleys hold fog cupped in their morning palms, across which a flurry of butterflies dances all summer. For the rhythm of weather, the turning of seasons and all the beauty that roots and renews. You were my community always—never leaving me, nor forsaking me. You are the soil from which I came and the soil to which I will go. I am soft clay scooped from the ground of your being.

To Winn Collier, Marilyn McEntyre, and John Blase, I express gratitude for nurturing my thoughts and words, for inspiring me with your own, and for introducing me to enduring literature during my Doctor of Ministry studies in the Sacred Art of Writing.

For Beth Stallinga and Katelyn DeVries and the bi-weekly lunches over which we discussed writing, great literature, and the state of the world, I give thanks.

Gratitude to Jim Dumerauf for reading the hard parts and talking me through the process of deciding what to share and what to keep to myself.

Special thanks to my high school English teacher, Mark Hiskes, who encouraged me in writing, ignited my love of books, and pointed my compass toward writing all those decades ago. Thank you for working through the manuscript and creating thoughtful questions for group dialogue around this book.

For the Holland United Church of Christ community, who has loved me through every hard and holy stretch, supporting me and celebrating the milestones with me. It must be said that without the HUCC community, the homecoming would have been hard and lonely.

This would not have been possible without the tireless efforts of Jeff Munroe and Steve Mathonnet-VanderWell, who believed in my story and felt it was worth sharing, and whose supreme editing skills made the whole thing top drawer, despite destroying all my adjectives and adverbs. 😊

I am grateful to David Crumm, Susan Stitt, and the team at Front Edge Publishing for their continual encouragement and support.

Gratitude to my friend and esteemed photographer, Jennifer Batts, for spending an evening with me around the back forty, capturing my love for the land of home in a way that helps tell the story. And Andrew Nelson, thank you for your beautiful videography for the book trailer.

About the Author

Christy Berghoef was raised on a generational forty-acre flower farm in Holland, Michigan. After receiving a Bachelor of Arts degree in Political Science from Calvin University, she moved to Washington, D.C., where she worked for a member of Congress. After growing dissatisfaction with the world of politics, she attended Calvin Theological Seminary.

After seminary, Christy and her husband Bryan began a ministry planting churches. While Bryan took the lead pastor role, Christy served as part-time worship coordinator while she and Bryan raised their four children. They have planted churches in Traverse City, Michigan; Washington, D.C.; and Holland, Michigan.

In addition, Christy has over a decade of experience speaking and consulting in the area of civil discourse, working with churches, schools, politicians, boards, businesses, and community groups. She also is a mindfulness practitioner and leads retreats and pilgrimages that focus on contemplation, mindfulness, and spiritual formation.

Much of her published writing has been in the areas of contemplation, nature, faith, and politics. She regularly writes on her Substack, which can be found at **christyberghoef. substack.com.**

Christy has a Doctor of Ministry degree in the Sacred Art of Writing from Western Theological Seminary and is the author of *Cracking the Pot.*

Christy enjoys contemplative photography, gardening, wandering in the woods, reading, writing poetry, and extended backpacking excursions around the globe. She sings, plays guitar and fiddle and writes music. Her books and photography can be found at **christyberghoef.com.**

She lives in Holland, Michigan, adjacent to the forty-acre flower farm of her childhood.

Telling Stories In The Dark
by Jeffrey Munroe

Millions live with sorrow, trauma, and grief. Jeffrey Munroe and a national array of experts explore true stories of resiliency, hope, and faith as people transform pain and find fresh inspiration.

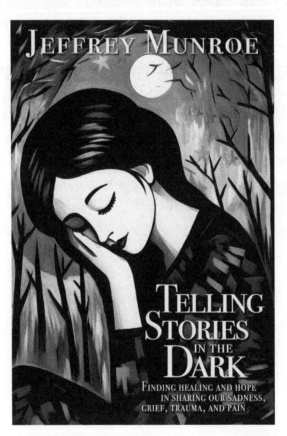

The Traveler's Path
by Douglas J. Brouwer

Travel defines us from our ancient spiritual roots to the movements of people around our planet today. Veteran traveler Douglas Brouwer invites us along on a wide range of journeys, inspiring us to embrace the transformative potential.

Green Street in Black and White
by Dave Larsen

In the early 1960s on Green Street, a boy and his friends face challenges in a neighborhood brimming with racial change. Dave Larsen takes us back to a summer of social upheaval, when youthful mischief collided with the weight of adult fears.

Reformed
Journal
Books

https://reformedjournal.com/all-books